The e-Revolution and Post-Compulsory Education

The best practices of e-business are revolutionising not just technology itself but the whole process through which services are provided; and from which important lessons can be learnt by post-compulsory educational institutions. This book aims to move debates about ICT and higher education beyond a simple focus on e-learning by considering the provision of post-compulsory education as a whole.

The e-Revolution and Post-Compulsory Education considers what we mean by e-business, why e-business approaches are relevant to universities and colleges and the key issues this raises for post-secondary education. The book:

- examines emerging technologies and provides examples of what an e-institution for education might look like;
- explores in depth what can be learnt from e-business in redefining the relationships between enterprises and their users, and in developing processes to improve services and competitive advantage;
- considers how to improve administrative efficiency, implement faster access and response to information, enhance skills and knowledge development, and improve the student experience;
- examines technological innovation and integration and the associated risk assessment and cost–benefit type analyses;
- explores issues in redesigning existing organisational frameworks, techniques for overcoming barriers to, and successfully implementing, change.

In a highly competitive educational marketplace, institutions need to react to, and embrace, new technologies to provide rich and competitive learning environments for the students of tomorrow. The discussion and guidance in this book will be essential reading for all leaders, managers and heads of e-learning in higher and further education.

Jos Boys is an independent e-learning consultant, based in the UK.

Peter Ford is now an Emeritus Professor and was Pro-Vice-Chancellor at the University of Nottingham.

The e-Revolution and Post-Compulsory Education

Using e-business models to deliver quality education

Edited by
Jos Boys and Peter Ford

In association with the Joint Information Systems Committee

Routledge
Taylor & Francis Group

LONDON AND NEW YORK

First published 2008
by Routledge
2 Park Square, Milton Park, Abingdon, Oxon OX14 4RN

Simultaneously published in the USA and Canada
by Routledge
270 Madison Avenue, New York, NY 10016

Routledge is an imprint of the Taylor & Francis Group, an informa business

© 2008 Higher Education Funding Council for England

Typeset in Sabon by
Florence Production Ltd, Stoodleigh, Devon
Printed and bound in Great Britain by
TJ International Ltd, Padstow, Cornwall

British Library Cataloguing in Publication Data
A catalogue record for this book is available
from the British Library

Library of Congress Cataloging in Publication Data
A catalog record for this book has been requested

ISBN10: 0-415-41986-7 (hbk)
ISBN10: 0-415-41987-5 (pbk)

ISBN13: 978-0-415-41986-4 (hbk)
ISBN13: 978-0-415-41987-1 (pbk)

Contents

Illustrations

Figures

Tables

Boxes

Contributors

Jos Boys
Independent e-learning consultant
Jos Boys was course leader for one of the first undergraduate programmes in the country to provide one laptop per student, which fully integrated ICT with face-to-face learning. She then worked as an instructional designer and researcher for the Centre for Educational and Technological Development at De Montfort University. In addition to co-authoring this book, Jos has undertaken several evaluation projects for the UK Joint Information Systems Committee (JISC) including *Managed Learning Environments: joined-up systems and the problems of organisational change*. She currently works as an academic developer and researcher at the University of Brighton.

William Buller
Internet Business Solutions Group, Cisco Systems, Inc.
William Buller has 20 years of experience implementing and consulting in information technology. Earlier in his career William focused on design, development and deployment of large-scale systems and was a founder member of the Price Waterhouse Cooper (PWC) Change Management Practice. More recently, William's work has been focused on e-business strategy deployment and the use of Internet technology to realise the business vision.

At Cisco, William is responsible for innovation in B2E as part of the Internet Business Solutions Group. In this role he works with many of Cisco's top 800 global customers to help them develop and realise their online employee vision within the context of their overall intranet strategy. This involves the development of new ideas, proving innovation in practice with customers and scaling solutions across all sectors within EMEA.

Michael Coen
Head of Innovation Services and Projects, Learning Services Department, University of Strathclyde
A Chartered management accountant by profession, Michael Coen has worked in the University's Information Resources Directorate, IT Services

Department and Finance Office, in addition to the Scottish Funding Council and the National Health Service. In recent years he has led a number of national and international research and development projects focusing on the use of information and related technologies in higher education. His interests include the design and implementation of information systems and encouraging the innovative and effective use of IT in education.

Peter Ford
Emeritus Professor, University of Nottingham
At various points in his career at the University Peter has held the posts of Director of Information Services, Head of the School of Computer Science and IT, Dean of Science, and Pro Vice-Chancellor. He continues to be Chairman of the National Computing Centre and EduServ Ltd, and is a non-executive director of a number of other companies concerned with Education or ICT. He also acts as an ICT consultant for many organisations across the world.

Graham Hill
Director of Management Information Services, University of Bradford
Graham Hill has been involved in developing, promoting and directing e-strategies (the virtual estate) within the university, resulting in significant new investments to complement the physical estates strategy. He chairs the University ICT Board and leads on administrative and academic information strategies. A past UCISA Chair of the Corporate Systems Group and an active member of UCISA committees, he is also involved in audit and consultancy relating to business systems implementation within UK higher education. He is an engineering graduate from Bristol University and has an MBA from the University of Bradford.

David Nicol
Director of e-Learning Research and Development, Centre for Academic Practice and Learning Enhancement (CAPLE), University of Strathclyde
Dr David Nicol currently leads a £1m e-learning transformation project funded by the Scottish Funding Councils. This is piloting improved models of assessment supported by technology across three Scottish universities. Recent research publications have focused on the social dimensions of e-learning, on learning objects, formative feedback including electronic feedback and on shared workspaces. David has developed and piloted institutional models for cost–benefit and risk analysis of e-learning investments with funding from JISC.

Daxa Patel
Freelance e-learning and e-business consultant
Daxa Patel is a freelance consultant, with a background in operations research, who previously worked for JISC in the UK as a Technology

Development Programmes Co-ordinator and as a Programme Director with specific responsibility for new technologies and standards, and for developing good practice in programme management and evaluation across JISC.

Prior to that she was employed at De Montfort University, where she fulfilled several roles. From 1997 to 2000 she worked within a team leading a strategic institutional change management initiative. Before that she was DMU's first ICT in Teaching and Learning Manager and developed the institution's first ICT in Teaching and Learning strategy. She also managed the institutional Teaching and Learning Projects programme.

Daxa set up the University Eurostudy Centre and has been a partner in several national and European e-learning projects (EOUN, WIRE, SAVIE). She co-authored *The Virtual University: the Internet and resource-based learning*, published by Kogan Page.

John Powell
Principal Lecturer, Dept of Strategy and Management, De Montfort University
John Powell has taught economics at De Montfort University since 1988 and in recent years has developed courses and e-learning materials in the areas of technology, innovation and e-business. He is programme leader for the BA e-Business Management degree and departmental 'evangelist' for e-learning, under JISC's e-Learning Capital Investment funding. John also has administrative responsibility for undergraduate admissions into the Faculty of Business and Law.

Karen Stanton
Chief Information Officer and College Librarian, King's College London
Until recently, Karen Stanton was Chief Information Officer at the University of Nottingham. Her role there included responsibility for the university's information technology infrastructure and information resources provision, including both library and ICT services. She had overall responsibility for developing information and knowledge management strategies. Karen has previously held senior information management roles at Sheffield Hallam University and the University of Birmingham. She is currently a member of several national bodies including the Knowledge Management Federation, the CIO Leadership Forum and the Standing Council of IT Directors. She acted as the University of Nottingham representative at Universitas 21 Information Services events and has recently worked with a number of overseas institutions to review IT developments.

Les Watson
Freelance education adviser
Les Watson is currently the lead consultant for the JISC Infonet project that produced the 'Developing Technology Rich Spaces for Learning' info-kit launched in March 2007. He was previously Pro-Vice-Chancellor

(Learning and Information Services) at Glasgow Caledonian University. He held this post from 1999 to September 2006. During this time he was responsible for Library, C and IT Services, student services, e-learning, the Caledonian Degree and work-based learning, all of which were integrated into a university-wide Learning Service. At Caledonian Les led the development of the Learning Cafe, REAL@Caledonian, and the award winning Saltire Centre.

Before this he was Dean of Learning and Information Services at the University of Gloucestershire where he previously held the post of Head of IT Services. Les started his career as a teacher of Biological Sciences in comprehensive schools in Hull and Gloucester before moving into higher Education as a Senior Lecturer in Computers in Education at Cheltenham and Gloucester College of Higher Education (now the University of Gloucestershire).

Preface

In 1996 a book was published entitled *Managing Change in Higher Education*. It sought to define a learning environment architecture that could be used to help universities manage the inevitable change towards e-learning. The introduction to that book stated:

> All providers of higher education today are faced with the challenge of building a system of higher education which will be equipped to meet the needs of society in the next century. The requirement to respond positively to change and to manage it effectively has never been so urgent. Universities and other institutions which provide higher education, are now subject to an unprecedented level of external scrutiny; the demands made of them have expanded, and the expectations have changed. Higher Education Institutions (HEIs) inhabit a more competitive world, where resources have become scarcer and where the impact of technology has never been so great or so unpredictable. They have entered global educational markets, while also forging local and regional links which are blurring the distinctions between study and employment and between different sectors of educational provision.
>
> (Ford *et al.* 1996:1)

Today these sentiments are still relevant; not just for higher education (HE) but for the whole of the post-compulsory education sector. The original book used a 'Learning Environment Architecture' to help with the implementation of change. This book aims to expand the horizons to embrace the whole spectrum of e-activities within the post-compulsory education sector across management, administration, learning support and teaching. With this wider scope the approach used before is not appropriate. Instead, the process by which this book has developed involved extensive dialogue with practitioners from HE and further education (FE) in the areas of pedagogy and support services, as well as management at many levels, and with key players from e-business. The intention is to explore whether and how developments in e-business can inform current and future practices in post-compulsory education.

This book is *not* trying to suggest that the UK HE and FE sectors should operate more like a commercial business. It *is* saying that universities and colleges can respond constructively to the intense commercial and other pressures they are now facing by exploiting the opportunities (and recognising the threats) offered by new technologies – in particular, Web-enabled information transfer and communication. It should also be emphasised that the authors are not advocating an e-business approach just because it is becoming technically feasible to do so, or that the *only* way forward is wholesale change. The exploration of e-business approaches in a post-compulsory educational context enables readers to consider a range of options. These can be pursued or rejected according to their own perception of the need for, and speed of, change within their own institutions. Nevertheless, the authors remain convinced that movement towards, and a critical understanding of, e-business approaches is important to help meet the future challenges of post-compulsory education provision.

Today, the World Wide Web forms a window onto all educational processes. The portal is now regarded as a powerful tool to allow unified Web access to hitherto unrelated data repositories, providing staff and students with quick, easy and comprehensive access to the information they require. Finance staff and administrators routinely use e-business tools in their day-to-day activities, and the need to support e-payment transactions for fees, bills, as well as salaries and wages, is now inevitable.

Evolving in parallel with business and learning needs are the various technologies that support them. Modern networks support the convergence of voice and data, allow image capture and transmission, and support an increasingly powerful range of multimedia learning tools. The roll-out of broadband access and the potential of wireless connectivity now take self-paced study and lifelong learning into a new era. Information exchange and communications become ever more integrated, faster and secure. Educational institutions need to respond to, and embrace, these new options to provide a rich and competitive learning environment for the students of tomorrow. These students will expect their portable or hand-held devices to integrate with the learning and administrative processes of their study and, in a highly competitive educational marketplace, those institutions that are slow to exploit the full potential of such evolving devices will inevitably lose market share. Of course, this does not mean 'throwing the baby out with the bathwater'. Existing traditional approaches to teaching and learning have many strengths and the e-revolution should be seen as complementary to these and offering enhancement to them, not as an alternative that will replace them.

At the same time, the emergence of the 'knowledge economy' will alter the profile and perceptions of the modern student as well as those of the teacher, researcher and administrator. The mobility of the student's studies through electronic credit transfer will become essential, with national and even international authenticated access to student data. Furthermore, the potential employability of the student will become increasingly tied in to the needs of the knowledge industry. All stakeholders (both within and outside the institution) will need to be very alive to the support needs, potential benefits and pitfalls that are associated with these issues.

These factors suggest that it is time to look beyond the mere automation of information (with administrative, academic and educational support functions still maintaining their separate functional silos) towards a more integrated and responsive system across a university's or college's processes, which rethinks what, where and how services are provided. This means both focusing more clearly on the institution's own core business and on building collaborations with others to share facilities, resources and services. There are many lessons to be learned here from the best of current e-business practices.

This book paints the picture of an e-institution from a variety of perspectives and charts a way forward from current situations. It was written by bringing together educational specialists from e-business, together with experts across HE and FE, from principals and pro-vice chancellors, to academics and researchers, to senior administrators and learning support staff. Substantial contributions were made by staff from IBM and Cisco systems. Several group meetings were held across the country to plan the structure of the book. From this beginning, some contributors wrote specific chapters while others gave valuable advice and guidance on drafts. We thank all of those involved in this process for their time and effort.

This book is aimed at senior managers in the HE and FE sectors, mainly in the UK but also elsewhere. It is intended to provide an outline of current developments in the e-business world and to provide an assessment from different viewpoints as to the value of these to universities and colleges. It does not try to offer one particular solution but to capture the state of play across various educational institutions, to share these and to look at potential ways forward.

The authors and other participants recognise the desirability for national government involvement to help with implementation of the suggested approaches outlined here. This book was facilitated by the Joint Information Systems Committee (JISC), which provides expertise and guidance in relation to information and communications technology (ICT) and the post-compulsory educational sector. Their support is much appreciated, as is that of the many senior academics and managers who have given their time to help with this book. The work here is just a beginning, which we hope will inform the important and continuing debate about how to manage post-compulsory education in an e-world.

Professor Peter Ford
Dr Jos Boys
December 2006

Bibliography

Peter Ford *et al.* (1996) *Managing Change in Higher Education: a learning environment architecture.* Society for Research into Higher Education and Open University Press.

Acknowledgements

In addition to the main contributors (listed on pp. ix-xii) the following people have been involved in the preparation of this book, through attending discussion groups, commenting on sections, providing information and offering critical overviews at various stages. We thank them all for their valuable support:

Roy Bailey, former Principal, Tynemouth College; Professor Sir Ron Cooke, Chair (JISC); Keith Duckitt, former Head of ICT, Learning and Skills Council; Andrew Dyson, Management and Leadership Programme Director, JISC; Judy Evans, Senior Assistant Registrar (Management Information), University of Brighton; Howard Freeman, Analyst programmer and instructional designer, FISI Ltd; Joyce Graves, Applications and Infrastructure, University of Nottingham; David House, Deputy Vice-Chancellor, University of Brighton; Mark Johnstone, Director of Learning, BBC Worldwide; Oleg Liber, Professor of e-Learning, Bolton Institute of Higher Education; Wen Lu, Oxford University Computing Sciences student; John Moore, Hyperbole Ltd; Nigel Peet, Director of Curriculum Support, South Cheshire College; Sarah Porter, JISC Head of Development; Paul Ricketts, Vice Principal, City College, Manchester; John Rockett, Principal, Rotherham FE College; Steve Ryan, Director, Centre for Learning Technology, London School of Economics; Professor Gilly Salmon, Professor of e-Learning, University of Leicester; Angela Telford, Director of Virtual Learning Centre, Tamworth and Lichfield College; Dr Heather Wharrad, Senior Lecturer, School of Nursing, Queens Medical Centre, University of Nottingham; Dr Caroline Windrum, Strategic Director, Learning Sciences Research Institute (LSRI), University of Nottingham.

Chapter 1

Introduction

Jos Boys

These days we are bombarded with stories of the successes – and failures – of the electronic revolution. From dot.coms to wi-fi, the ways in which we get information, communicate with each other and engage in business are being transformed. Post-compulsory education – in all its different forms – is responding to these changes, and in some cases may be at the forefront of innovative development, particularly in the use of electronic media and networking for learning and teaching. But where post-compulsory education in the UK does lag behind the best practices of e-enterprise is in engaging with the implications of information and communications technology (ICT) for the whole nature of its services. This book argues that it is now becoming urgent for universities and colleges to grapple with the implications of ICT beyond simply automating existing processes, by understanding how new technologies enable better integration of university and college systems across the traditional divide of academic and administrative services.

Why, then, should we look to e-business practices as a place to learn lessons about new technologies for educational provision? I suggest there are several reasons:

- The clear divide between 'business' and 'educational' provision is blurring, such that post-compulsory providers are now not only competing with other universities and colleges both in the UK and globally, but also with company-based and other private services. Universities and colleges can learn from the different approaches these competitors have taken.
- There are important lessons to be learnt from contemporary changes in the business world, as relationships between customer, product and service are increasingly redefined – often, it will be proposed as something that is more like the long-term student/college relationship, rather than mere buy/sell transactions.
- Post-compulsory education is under huge financial pressure and needs to operate more effectively and more cheaply. Although ICT per se is

not an immediate panacea to this problem, the integration of systems
that new technologies enable and the related rethinking of organisational
roles and services can offer benefits.

- Government and other funders are increasingly emphasising employability, both for vocational training and for 'knowledge' workers. ICT
is already a core part of the capabilities demanded from our graduates
and this trend can only continue.
- Post-compulsory education is under pressure to make its information
resources, data management processes and transactions more 'businesslike'. Effective, well-designed and integrated e-systems can both support
a university's or college's educational objectives and meet these demands
for better reporting and data tracking.

E-approaches are already well established in the post-compulsory
education sector in the UK. Here, in order to build on that experience, we
need to consider, first, why e-business approaches are relevant to universities
and colleges, second, what we mean by e-business, and third, the key issues
this raises for educational services provision.

Why look at e-business?

Most commentators agree that the ubiquity of the Internet and the emergence of ever-new ICTs is transforming older forms of business enterprise.[1]
In addition to Web-enabled networks, we now have ever increasing computer power in smaller and cheaper packages and high-speed broadband
connectivity via a plethora of services and devices. All of this is enabling
information storage and transfer of all sorts to be faster, more integrated,
more customised and accessible anywhere, anytime. At the same time, vastly
expanding virtual networks are enabling new forms of competition and
collaboration and enhancing consumer knowledge. The impact of this on
how businesses organise themselves and provide services is already far-
reaching.

First, many businesses no longer simply provide products *or* services
but instead offer an integration of products *and* services, aimed at fulfilling
a wide range of needs and desires. In this process service providers and
consumers are no longer separate but part of an interconnected Web of
economic, information and social exchange. Buying and selling transactions
have become more customer-centred, and with much more integrated and
long-term linkages to associated services. Products can be 'mass-customised'
and services truly personalised, with a much more interactive relationship between supplier and customers, and between customers themselves.

Second, organisations are becoming much more adaptable, flexible and
less 'corporate', with even competitors learning to collaborate for mutual
benefit. Where one institution begins and another ends is much more blurred

as expertise is shared and/or outsourced. E-businesses focus on their core competencies and differentiating capabilities.

Third, organisational roles are also much more flexible, related to changing requirements rather than fixed job descriptions, with built-in on-the-job continuous professional development and training. This enables organisations to be much more responsive to dynamic and unpredictable change and to the needs of their customers and partners. Similarly, supporting infrastructures are moving beyond a conventional client/server model to more flexible, intelligent (and open source) technologies, which also can respond to change quickly and effectively.

Finally, personal communication devices (laptops, mobiles, PDAs, etc.) are becoming ubiquitous and multi-modal, requiring hardware and software technologies that enable interoperability and offer the potential of consumer choice across media and access modes. In parallel, communication software and tools are becoming more customer focused; with the next generation of Web-enabled services – Web 2.0 applications – being very much based on social interaction and the mass sharing of materials (for example, easily usable Web-blog tools, social fora such as MySpace and the sharing of photographs via Flickr or videos via YouTube).

Post-compulsory educational institutions are beginning to locate themselves in relation to these changes. This is not a simple process. Most post-compulsory education in the UK is not a commercial business. It is not financed in the same way nor is its public provision framed only by the profit motive. As I have already noted, education is also more like the blurred customer–supplier relationship that businesses are just beginning to notice. But are we clear about whether to conceptualise students as the clients, consumers, customers, employees, members or 'something else' of an educational institution? And how does that affect how we provide services? Universities and colleges are also exploring the implications of competition versus collaboration and the pros and cons of outsourcing or sharing non-core elements. They may be buying in cleaning and catering services. They may be franchising educational services to other institutions, providing accreditation to courses supplied elsewhere or developing new campuses globally. They are doing this in a marketplace that is increasingly global, challenged by other educational suppliers (both public and private), hedged around by government requirements and under tight financial constraints. How, then, in a risk-averse environment, can HE and FE education respond to opportunities through using ICT strategically, creatively and flexibly?

In the early days of the Internet, through the introduction of JANET and SUPERJANET, UK universities and colleges were at the forefront of the information revolution. All are now engaged in improving ICT infrastructures, hardware and connectivity – trying to keep up with the speed of technological change, within tight budgets. Most have some kind of e-learning provision, often linked to a management information system (MIS) or are implementing a managed learning environment (MLE). Many continue to innovate, particularly in the area of e-learning. However, the limitations of just automating a MIS or working from e-learning 'outwards' are becoming increasingly clear. Such an approach is not enabling educational institutions to think holistically about the services they provide to staff and students. Aspects of provision are tinkered with, piecemeal adaptations made, gaps and duplications perpetuated. Instead, we need to use the impact of emerging ICTs as an opportunity to rethink the *whole* business of education. Over ten years ago, Ernst *et al.* (1994) proposed that emerging technologies would enable HE to have *different* strategies to deal with reductions in resources and other changing trends, compared to their more traditional methods. These are listed under four imperatives (see Figure 1.1), which remain highly relevant.

This book argues that the best e-business approaches suggest ways of making such strategic-level shifts to an organisation, underpinned by the capabilities of new ICTs. The impact of such rethinking will vary considerably from institution to institution. In some cases it may result in only minor shifts, in others more radical change. Here, we aim to show some potential ways forward.

What is e-business?

What, then, do we mean by e-business and how is it relevant to the challenges faced by the post-compulsory education sector at the beginning of the twenty-first century? Most obvious is the potential for productivity gains offered by both the speeding up and the integration of communication and data. Individuals from different departments, organisations and countries can work efficiently together sharing knowledge and information across both functional and physical boundaries. Even more importantly, their customers and other stakeholders can access relevant information and communicate their requirements quickly, accurately and from any location. The term e-business – whatever its precise definition – means more than this, however. It is about building these key capabilities of speed and integration into the whole business process. Although there are different ways of interpreting this, the framework used in this book (see Chapter 3) is through the key issues of customer focus, organisational integration and common systems.

Customer focus

Business processes, applications and systems need to be designed to put the customer at the centre – to create added value by giving them more easily accessible, timely and relevant information and by giving them more control

Imperative: increase administrative productivity	
Adhocratic	Planning centric
Cut expenses across the board	■ Develop a vision ■ Identify academic priorities ■ Rethink mission/markets ■ Nurture Internal growth sectors
Cut administration deeper	■ Redefine administration ■ Eliminate unnecessary work ■ Dismantle unproductive policy ■ Reengineer processes ■ Leverage the IT infrastructure ■ Attack paperwork
Tighten procedures and seek scale through centralisation	■ Empower employees ■ Leverage the private market ■ Embed procedural controls in IT infrastructure

Imperative: enhance controls and reporting	
Old strategies	Emergent strategies
■ Introduce new rules ■ Introduce new forms ■ Acquire additional signatures ■ Centralise approval authority	■ Specify desired outcomes ■ Negotiate acceptable risk ■ Embed controls in IT ■ Measure and elevate continually

Imperative: adopt a consumer orientation	
Old strategies	Emergent strategies
■ Do things right ■ Assure compliance ■ Foster specialisation ■ Manage by exception ■ Safeguard institutional data	■ Do the right things, right ■ Become a problem solver ■ Empower generalists ■ Create centres of competency ■ Promote access to information

Imperative: facilitate organisational change	
Old strategies	Emergent strategies
■ Add vertical layers ■ Enhance vertical communications ■ Create functional 'stovepipes' ■ Use the chain of command	■ Create a network of networks ■ Reduce information float ■ Promote cross-functional integration ■ Use the network

Figure 1.1 New business imperatives.
Source: Ernst *et al.* 1994.

over their own data. Although students may not be customers in the conventional market sense, their position at the centre of educational services means that they have an analogous role. Chapters 4 and 6 will address this issue in greater detail, arguing that students (and other stakeholders) are more like 'members' of an organisation than just its customers. It will show how some types of e-businesses have developed a 'community' model, based on user loyalty, and are already using the membership concept to enhance the quality and value of their services.

New technologies support customer/member focus because they enable data to be widely and commonly shared and to be precisely customised for and by each user. This may be by being able to make and track transactions online. It may be by enabling all kinds of formal and informal communications between users. It may be by exploiting the capacity to share data between customers, as with Amazon's book peer-review service. It may be by enabling people to amend their own personal data directly or share, add to and learn from a constantly updating online knowledge repository. The Guardian Unlimited online travel section, for example, enables readers to write and share reviews of holiday destinations, to share travel tips with others and to upload photographs. Where these ICT innovations work well the customer experience is enhanced and the business can also achieve productivity gains and competitive advantage.

Organisational integration

Electronic networks can now operate quickly and securely across functions, locations and conventional organisational boundaries, enabling both new patterns of collaboration and of customisation. Data can be communicated much more efficiently, while types and degrees of access can be carefully controlled – both by being tailored to different requirements and in terms of robust security. This has implications for how a business runs itself, the roles of the individuals within it and how it collaborates with others elsewhere. Such organisational integration requires a holistic and strategic approach. It must be based on making flexible and multi-layered relationships across and beyond the usual boundaries of separate organisations (or departments or faculties) and between administrative, learning support and academic staff, students, suppliers and other stakeholders.

Common systems

For this seamless integration of data to happen, underlying systems that need to communicate to each other will increasingly need to be standardised or at least be compatible. This is essential in terms of business process, data management and communication. Thus, organisational integration has to be underpinned with appropriate business systems and ICT infrastructure. Educational institutions will need increasingly to differentiate between core services demanding common systems and standards, and more autonomous and less central activities, where separate operation does not impact on the effectiveness and connectivity of the organisation as a whole.

What, then, are the key issues in the relationships between a post-compulsory educational institution and the best e-business approaches? Three main themes underpin the different contributions to this book:

E-business approaches and post-compulsory education:
What do we mean by e-business approaches? In what ways might these be relevant to post-compulsory education? What kind of e-business is education?

Changing contexts:
What are the UK and global contexts for post-compulsory education that are affecting how universities and colleges can respond to revolutionary changes in ICT?

Improving educational services:
How are universities and colleges already using ICT to support their goals? How can post-compulsory education use new ICT technologies to improve its service to 'customers'? How will this affect organisational structures and roles? And what supporting technologies and standards are required?

Each of these will be briefly outlined in turn.

E-business approaches and post-compulsory education

Post-compulsory education in the UK is under constant pressure. It needs to respond quickly to changing contexts, whether economic, political or social. It must also predict and then adapt to the changing shape of the student body, to their study requirements and to shifts in employment and the economy. In addition, its public providers sit between the public and private sectors, and will have objectives that are not merely about cost effectiveness but also about ethics and the wider public interest. These are not easy tasks. But, at the same time, post-compulsory education is failing to learn lessons from the wider business world, partly because of a history of considerable ambivalence about the relationship of education to business. Post-compulsory education is objectively under many commercial and financial pressures, but at the same time its practitioners often resist any suggestion that it might be more 'businesslike'. As Milton Greenberg puts it:

The underlying premise is that the application of managerial practices (i.e. personnel and fiscal controls known as 'administration') in the conduct of the academic enterprise will infiltrate faculty prerogatives and restrict the freedom to teach and learn. Faculty are the protectors and explicators of the true faith which must be defended against potential infidels, including their own administrators, who 'think about nothing but money'.

(2004: 3)

Some argue that this is because of a self-referential model of (particularly higher) education, basing its objectives only on the inwardly centred cycles of subject discipline and academic autonomy. De Long writes:

Professors do their research and teach classes for job-oriented under-graduate students who continue to be marketable to employers – where else would they recruit? The university improves its 'service' under the rubric of recruitment and retention, in order to maintain market share. Occasionally a superior student comes along who is nurtured in the scholarly ways and then hired to replenish the ranks of the professoriate. For those on the inside, it is a self-sustaining, self-contained world.

(1997–8: 15)

Greenberg argues that this common reaction to 'business' from academics is due to confusion between the *substance* of teaching, learning and research, which is (and should be) protected by academic freedom and professional standards and the *processes* through which these activities are undertaken; for example, in the continuing – and unnecessary – assumption that university education can only be provided by having thousands of teachers of differing skills across the country in many different places, teaching and assessing self-selected variations on a discipline theme.

As already stated, this book is not suggesting that learning from e-business is about making education more commercial and profit-driven. Defining the *substance* of teaching, learning and research services is exactly about understanding the core business of a particular university or college. Here, learning from e-business is about being willing to change those aspects of educational provision that are not – ultimately – supporting customer focus (for example, in having complex, time-consuming enrolment procedures where students must queue for hours); that work against organisational integration (such as the continuing tendency to functional divisions and a 'silo' mentality); and that prevent common systems and standards where these could improve services to students (such as when the historically accumulative patterns of departmental autonomy remain embedded and go on preventing effective sharing of data).

In the early days of the Internet, many believed that e-learning would develop quickly to overtake face-to-face contact and would 'inevitably' revolutionise post-compulsory education. This hasn't happened for a variety of reasons. Instead we have moved towards what has been called 'hybrid', 'enhanced' and 'blended' learning in universities and colleges, that is, where e-learning systems and materials supplement rather than replace campus-based study. Rather than merely extolling the benefits of e-learning, in this book we are interested in exploring the implications of a whole variety of potential learning modes.[2] Table 1.1 summarises four kinds of relationships between online and conventional forms of teaching and learning that are now becoming common. Chapter 4 will consider the e-business characteristics of these different combinations in greater detail.

Gary Matkin has analysed e-learning trends and pressures (in the US context) and found a range of approaches; from classroom enhancement, through to virtual universities developed as separate entities, as new internal units, through consortia, as non-profit and for-profit spin-offs and via partnerships with for–profit organisations (Matkin 2002: 10). The 2001 University of California conference 'University Teaching as e-Business; Research and Policy Agendas', of which Matkin's contribution was part, provided some useful case studies for examining these different partnering combinations. As Goldstein notes, there are multiple variations possible:

> we are seeing a hybridisation of providers, of non-profits that are partnering or creating for-profits, of public institutions that are partnering or creating for-profit entities.
>
> (2002: 13)

Table 1.1 Educational strategies, service provision and typical market

Educational strategy	Service	Market
Distance learning	Instructor led *or* content led Individual or cohort-based Asynchronous delivery	Convenience (anytime, anywhere) Part-time
Hybrid (combination of online learning and classroom-based study)	Instructor-led *or* content-led Individual and cohort-based Synchronous and asynchronous delivery	Flexibility Mixed-mode
Blended (online materials supplement face-to-face learning)	Instructor-led Cohort-based Synchronous and asynchronous delivery	Service enhancement Full-time and part-time
Traditional learning	Instructor-led Cohort-based Synchronous delivery	Experience Full-time and part-time

Source: adapted from Matkin 2002.

He suggests that many of these new collaborations were generated by the assumed importance of three things: of branding (citing UNext's Cardean University, an online organisation that attempted co-branding by linking to four highly regarded American universities); of quality, meaning large-scale investment in content, which has yet to be proven to generate related returns; or of price, with some competitors deliberately aiming for the low-end of the market (see Chapter 5). However, he suggests that, ultimately, convenience and service to the student have most impact in attracting and holding customers:

> Where Phoenix (Online) is really, really good, and where most other institutions are really, really bad – and what we are learning really, really counts – is student service. We have had a lot of examples of institutions coming up with really good models of learning, and really good content, really well presented, and yet it fails to hold an audience. And the reason it fails to hold the audience is that when the student called with a question, nobody answered . . . in this regard, on-line is no different from the campus – a long registration line, whether snaking across the gym or while placed on hold, is a long line. And students hate it.
> (Goldstein 2002: 14–15)

In the UK, the adding of an 'e' to educational services has tended to con-centrate on quality enhancement, that is, as hybrid or blended learning, based on the addition of high-quality Web-based content to support traditional teaching. Unfortunately, there remains a basic contradiction here when this version of provision is combined with scarce resources and an autonomous instructor-led model of education. Individual academics are being asked to design high quality, online materials, but without the supporting expertise or resources. And their efforts most often merely go towards one particular course or module, that is, are not used many times. This, I would suggest, is not a workable business model for the long-term development of effective e-learning. It can be expensive, it does not guarantee quality and it is not scaleable.[3] Chapter 5 will explore attempts to improve the expansion and reuse of e-learning materials within UK universities and colleges. But as Sally Johnstone writes:

> If you are just doing what we usually do in higher education, running the technology project like a cottage industry with a single faculty member serving a group of students, it doesn't work too well in terms of ultimate cost. You also tend to burn out the faculty member.
> (Johnstone 2002: 17–20)

As the Open Universities worldwide have shown for over 25 years, changing the type of educational service also demands different organisational models. The Open University (OU) in Britain invests in the design of good courseware by specialists – both academic and learning technologists – which is then taught across many sites, by correspondence and online, by teaching assistants. Not surprisingly, the conclusion of the University of California, Berkeley conference already mentioned is that, to date, it is provision of e-learning as a separate facility (whether as an autonomous in-house unit, partnership or as a new entity) that has been most successful for universities and colleges in business terms. This is mainly because it has provided not-for-profit educational institutions with a means to 'sidestep' the inherent difficulties caused by current assumptions about academic autonomy and control. To really integrate e-learning as a valuable asset for students and teachers alike in HE and FE, we may need to learn from aspects of private sector provision. This is not about undermining that autonomy; it is about rethinking institutional processes and organisational roles. As Johnstone goes on to say:

> How do we sort through institutional models that can support the roles of individuals to make the use of these technologies feasible? The structure we have now really just doesn't work. We need to shift traditional faculty roles. We need to create additional definitions for professionals working within higher education on the teaching and learning process. We also need to balance what that means in terms of status and costs to the institution that is supporting them.
>
> (2002: 17)

Post-compulsory education in a changing context

In the British context it is probably the further education sector that is feeling the most immediate pressures from commercial education providers. As of 2007, the UK government made it compete directly with private education providers for funding. Requiring FE colleges to operate against private provision is not new. Contestability – competition based on quality and price – is already happening; the key difference is that a slice of public funds (between 5 and 10 per cent) will be bid for in direct competition with private providers for the first time. In addition, as Francis Beckett put it in *The Guardian* newspaper:

> Meanwhile, the work on delivering Train to Gain – the programme of free workplace training – will be handed out to a network of brokers, to be appointed by the Learning and Skills Council. The brokers will find out what employers want and commission workplace training to provide it. Colleges will be competing with companies to win over brokers.
>
> (21 March 2006: 9)

As part of a process of making the FE sector more competitive, it has refocused on the 16–19 age group and individual colleges have collaborated and consolidated across regional areas. Such shifts may indicate potential changes across the post-compulsory sector as a whole. The UK government has already shown itself interested in public–private partnering, competition and in funding the private sector directly for services in other areas such as healthcare, schools and nurseries. There has also been a considerable growth in corporate universities, employer-led training and private education providers in the last few years; and an increasing take-up of their courses and training packages. For universities, both the competition and the potential for collaborative partnerships is most clearly seen in a global rather than a regional context. New alliances across national boundaries being attempted in many instances (see Chapter 5). In this context, universities and colleges need to have a clear idea of what they want their educational model to be, what kind of 'brand identity' they have (or could have) and how to offer high quality, appropriate and cost effective educational services in a world where the e-revolution is becoming the norm.

What kind of e-business is education?

What, then, are alternative institutional models for these new hybrid forms of post-compulsory education? The e-business approach argues for defining core and subsidiary processes. Here, as an indication, I suggest that we might generically define the essential elements of the sector as:

- the provision of educational services;
- the granting of awards for educational achievement;
- the development of academic subject knowledge.

Yet these processes are not explicitly business- or even customer–driven; that is, they centre on knowledge and skills (and their validation), not on profit or loss. Even with the introduction of fees in the UK, there is no direct transactional relationship between applicant, student and tutor or specific service. Even applying to university is intermediated by UCAS. In this sense, education is *not* a straightforward business. At the same time, post-compulsory education has obligations to a whole range of stakeholders, from government agencies, local education authorities and taxpayers through to its own customers and staff. All these groups have a legitimate interest in defining what kind of outcomes they expect universities and colleges to achieve, which may be at odds with how these services are defined and provided from within the institution. Research by Cunningham and Hood (1997) into these different perceptions outlines some of these conflicts and contradictions but also summarises what academic and other stakeholder perspectives share:

- courses should be reputable;
- students should be able to get jobs in their area of study;
- quality of life of a graduate should be enhanced by the university experience;
- graduates should contribute to the community both economically and socially;
- courses should make good use of resources;
- post-compulsory education should be available to all qualified citizens;
- knowledge has a central role in the mission of the university.

Education, then, is predominantly an 'experience' good, engaged with over a relatively long period of time, and not simply a product that can be consumed (see Chapter 4). I have already suggested that students might be seen more as members than customers of a particular educational institution. It is also clear that although there may be conflicts of interest over what the educational process is *for* (such as education for employment 'versus' education for life) the element of ethical and public service remains popular and strong. This framework, however, does not preclude post-compulsory education from having business drivers and objectives, some of which are listed in Table 1.2, adapted from the work of Dolence and Norris (1995).

Table 1.2 Example business drivers and objectives for post-compulsory education

Example drivers	Example objectives
Cost pressures	Increase productivity Reduce costs Find new income streams Outsource non-central activities Improve retention, progression and achievement
Increased student expectations	Find new competitive advantage Improve facilities Improve student experience Add value to existing services
Increased competition	Improve brand identity Collaborate in areas of expertise Focus on specific markets
Increased regulation	Improve performance targets and measures Enhance performance monitoring and improvement processes

Source: adapted from Dolence and Norris 1995.

This book will explore the lessons we can learn from e-business in order to respond creatively and constructively to the challenges of business objectives such as these. It will show how new information and communication technologies offer not just tools to support change, but also new kinds of *models* and *processes*.

Chapter 5 will explore what universities and colleges are already doing in integrating ICT into their everyday activities. Here, we need next to consider briefly how post-compulsory education can use new technologies to improve its service to 'customers'. How will this affect organisational structures and roles? And what supporting technologies and standards are required?

How can post-compulsory education improve its service to 'customers'?

Many academic and administrative staff may well argue that we already put students at the centre of our activities. The most immediate response is that many university and college services are often still more focused on their internal and departmental objectives and are poorly integrated across the institution, making the student experience of the 'whole' fragmented, complicated and confusing. At the same time academics often have multiple individual goals and may be overloaded or under-resourced, potentially forced into limited or distracted relationships with students. Poor retention statistics are often an indicator that where problems arise, non-integrated knowledge of performance allows students to fall through the net and drop out.

It will be argued here that the best e-business practices can enable us to rethink both the student experience and student–staff relationships beyond just additive improvements to what already happens. It is about making educational services much more flexible and adaptive to their customers. Table 1.3 indicates some of the ways in which an e-business oriented education might differ from conventional patterns. Here, individual transactions between staff, students, suppliers and stakeholders are not functionally separate events, but fully integrated whether educational, management or financial. Services are not a 'one-way' delivery from institution to student, but start from the student experience (as part of a longer term and increasingly reciprocal relationship between enquirer, applicant, student, alumni and lifelong learner).

More detailed considerations of an appropriate educational student experience for an e-world are discussed throughout this book.

Table 1.3 Conventional and e-business models of post-compulsory education

Conventional	e-Business oriented
Provider driven	Learner driven
Single institution study	Multiple provider and locational/ networked opportunities
Minimum entry standards, progression by level, minimum attainment standards	Entry, progression and achievement on demonstration of mastery
'One course suits all'	Multiple outcomes
Set whole cohort timetables and access	Customised, anywhere, anytime access
Education compartmentalised from employment	Integrated and lifelong learning
Fragmented services across academic, learning support and administrative areas	Seamless, student-oriented support via Web portal

Source: adapted from Dolence and Noriss 1995.

How will this affect organisational structures and roles?

Such an approach has many implications for how colleges and universities are organised. First, institutions need to consider what facilities and services they provide 'in-house' and what is better achieved via out-sourcing or collaboration. What is their 'core' business and what is peripheral? How might they collaborate with other institutions to integrate aspects of the student's experience while separating out who supplies what? This 'multiple provider' model could have major implications for how, and where, students study and who awards their degrees.

Second, they need to rationalise their services as common and integrated processes. The e-business approach can only work where these core functions are not separate 'bunkers' using different systems, but work to agreed processes and standards. Finally, they need to explore making provision more customer-oriented and 'self-service' where appropriate. Table 1.4 indicates how roles might be considered differently.

What supporting technologies and standards are required?

Although the predicted shift to e-learning and the virtual university has not yet come to pass, and students (and staff) continue to prefer studying in real buildings with real people, emerging technologies continue to have implications not just for teaching and learning but for the 'business' of

Table 1.4 Conventional and e-business organisational structures and roles for post-compulsory education

Conventional	e-Business oriented
Matching institutional and operational boundaries	Flexible relationships with competitors and collaborators
Rigid academic, administrative and departmental roles	Staff flexibility, mobility and ongoing CPD
Bureaucratic, inflexible and rule-driven procedures	Flexible and customised services
Separate, functionally organised	Integrated and hybrid process-oriented
Multiple, non-compatible processes	Seamless, appropriate access to data

Source: adapted from Dolence and Norris 1995.

education as a whole. Web-enabled high-speed networks, coupled with increasing computer power, enable effective, robust and secure data integration and transfer, where these are supported with common standards and processes. Increasingly we are moving beyond a simple client/server model, where applications and hardware form a single bundle, towards more dynamic and flexible service-oriented architecture (see Chapter 9). Most post-compulsory educational institutions are already beginning to face up to these issues. They are making MIS systems more integrated, moving towards unified security and authentication processes, and developing portals to provide a single point of access to information. In the FE sector, in particular, networks linking colleges regionally are already in place in some cases. Again, we can look to Dolence and Norris (1995) for an outline of how understandings of ICT are changing (see Table 1.5).

The future(s) for post-compulsory education

I have argued that, in important ways, HE and FE provision is different to mainstream business, and that learning from e-business is not about becoming a fully commercial organisation but about finding ways of responding constructively to the competition from private education providers as well as other pressures. The similarities and differences between post-compulsory education and e-business approaches need to be thought through. Some differences are important and will affect what types of lessons can be learnt. Others are just the accumulated result of tradition and practice – the cultural and historical baggage of post-compulsory education – which is working against improved forms of educational provision. How, for example, do we relate to assumptions of academic autonomy, so strongly

Table 1.5 Conventional and e-business technologies for post-compulsory education

Conventional	e-Business oriented
Classroom, lab and library with technological aids as 'add-ons'	ICT embedded and network oriented
Client/server infrastructure	On demand, flexible provision, through a variety of devices and network modes
Single mode delivery	Customised multi-modal choice (voice, text, graphic)
Separate databases and reporting with limited statistics and monitoring	Immediate, updating statistics and multiple forms of reporting
Poor market knowledge/slow response times	Good market intelligence/continuous improvement

Source: adapted from Dolence and Norris 1995.

held in HE (but not in FE) or the emphasis on research in the old universities, but not in post-1992 institutions? How much should we reorganise older functional departments and integrate researchers, academics, student support services and administrators?

Moving whole institutions towards much more integrated systems remains a difficult task. Most post-compulsory educational institutions are necessarily risk-averse. The process of implementing appropriate and integrated technologies can be costly and time-consuming and mistakes difficult to unravel. For business, the implementation of e-commerce is often critical to operations and survival. For university and college management its benefits may seem less obvious, and its development uncertain. In addition, some innovations can only occur from a nationwide or government initiative (particularly in terms of aligning common standards). The Signposter project, for example, aims to provide a single service for integrating educational information and learning opportunities for individuals into one national database (see Box 1.1). UniTEST is a generic university admissions test being developed (separate to current admissions processes of A levels and other prior qualifications) to assist universities in making admissions decisions and widen participation in higher education. Offered jointly by ACER and Cambridge Assessment, the providers argue that such a generic test 'can be used to make student selection and recruitment fairer than it is already, whilst bringing greater transparency to the admissions process.' (ACER and Cambridge Assessment 2006).

Although this book is committed to the central lessons and implications of good e-business practices – customer focus, organisational integration and common systems – it is not arguing that all universities and colleges need to redefine their every process. Some may introduce change in specific

Box 1.1 Signposter
The commercially viable free information service for individual learners

Signposter is intended to provide free access to up-to-date relevant and complete information to individual learners from the age of 14 upwards. The service will reach all parts of the education sector including the emerging corporate university market and provide a unified learning and support service that includes, for example, advice about funding bodies in a sector that currently lacks coherence and is becoming more complex.

To avoid confusion it will be a unique system without competitors and will generate revenue from other activities such as advertising and sponsorship and not be funded by government grants. Signposter is a private–public partnership project and will attract investors from both sectors. The benefit is that it will deliver a level of service to investing partners at lower cost than they could achieve individually.

The system will provide mainstream access to comprehensive information through the national virtual network that Signposter will build in keeping with the recommendation of the Morrison Report. For example, if a learner requires an online course or materials the individual can register and pay for these resources, complete the course and do the assessment without coming out of the Signposter service. For institutions seeking to harness staff or courses, Signposter provides a route to market.

A self-diagnostic system will encourage learners to develop their own personal e-portfolio (learning profile), which will underpin a lifetime of learning. This is an intelligent system that will help the individual to select the most appropriate options and to recognise relevant opportunities to future learning. E-portfolio satisfies the QAA requirement that undergraduates have a personal training programme.

Signposter will be built on the 'Google model' by Signposter's technology partners, Fujitsu and Oracle.

How will services be resourced?
Information sources and content will come from a strategic network of alliances and partnerships. Significant areas are already covered by WorkTrain, learndirect, HotCourses and HEFCE, but additional resources are needed. These will come from professional bodies, chartered institutes, Sector Skills Councils Network, private sector job agencies and awarding and examining bodies.

There are many initiatives currently seeking to provide networked solutions to meet the various needs of government, education and employment, but the national virtual infrastructure will need to come from non-government sources that are not centrally controlled and Signposter will play a key role in the realisation of this national resource.

areas only. Systems only need to be rationalised and common where sharing takes place; otherwise these can remain autonomous (see Chapter 3). Although most of what follows can be taken as relevant to both the HE and FE sectors in the UK, it will also be important to underline key differences and their implications. The FE sector is a huge and growing component of post-compulsory provision and is structured very differently to HE. In addition, we do not wish to blur some of the real differences between pre- and post-1992 UK universities. Each institution is therefore likely to prioritise their business drivers and objectives in different ways. This book is not offering a 'single' solution. It is up to each institution to understand its own business drivers and objectives and to implement relevant and appropriate improvements.

Levels of change

Throughout this book, we will use the MIT 90s model to define different levels in the use of technologies and their impact on customer focus, organisational integration and systems rationalisation. The MIT 90s programme took place in the early 1990s and involved 32 research projects and 40 research staff based at the Massachusetts Institute of Technology. The programme analysed the use of ICT in a number of business organisations. In the early 2000s we might think that such a model is a bit long in the tooth and no longer applicable. However, although much has happened in the years since this research was undertaken, the basic truths of the potential of ICT remain and are only fully exploited in some places and not others. It is a generic model, not tied to the implementation of any specific ICT architecture.

It is appropriate that the MIT 90s model is a descriptive one, as ICT impact and returns are often intangible. The model identifies five phases of success with ICT, which range from localised to innovative use. These phases are grouped into two stages. Stage 1, (with phases one and two) is regarded as an evolutionary stage covering a phase of 'localised use of ICT' leading to an 'internal integration' of use of ICT. Stage 2, regarded as revolutionary, has phases covering 'business process redesign', to 'business network redesign' and finally 'business scope redefinition'. The MIT 90s model is therefore clearly a business-centred model and as such supports our consideration of HE and FE institutions as e-businesses.

In considering how the MIT 90s model could be applied to the use of ICT in education, the National Council for Educational Technology (NCET – now Becta) further developed the model by identifying an additional stage, but retaining, although renaming, the five phases. In the NCET version of the model for educational ICT (see Figure 1.2), a transformative stage is identified. Redesigning business processes (as this phase is called in the original model) is clearly potentially transformational. However, expressing this as transformation rather than referring to business processes directly

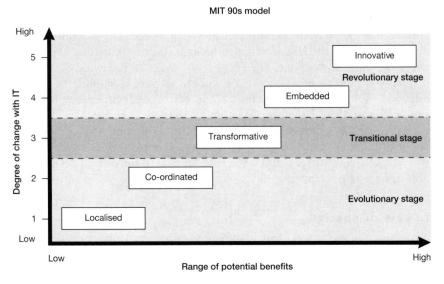

Figure 1.2 MIT 90s model of levels of technological change.

Source: adapted from Scott Morton 1991.

is likely to be more palatable to many in the education sector. Transformation is currently a hot topic for education. The application of ICT in a way that acknowledges the essentially human nature of the enterprise and includes preparing people to 'exploit the new functionality' is what College Boards of Management and University Courts are striving to achieve.

The underlying assumption in this model is that the more ICT transforms an organisation, the greater the benefit to it. It is clear that the preliminary stages of localised and co-ordinated use are likely to involve automation of current processes whereas the higher levels of use are focused on embedding the use of ICT and developing innovative new processes. Of interest here is the transformational stage that involves the development of new processes that do things differently. This is the famous 'tipping point' identified by Malcolm Gladwell (2000), where a small subtle shift in the mix of factors in a situation is sufficient to 'tip' the system to produce a transformation. That difference in our context is when ICT actually starts to have a real effect on the organisation's institutional performance.

It is also clear, and this has considerable bearing on the success or failure to get real benefit from IT in education, that the early phases can be achieved with the hard work and commitment of individual members of staff. The ICT evangelist and his or her friends can make phases 1 and 2 a reality. A phase 1 example might be developing blended learning within a department. A phase 2 example might be aspects of an MLE. However, the later stages, because they involve organisation-wide processes such as business process redesign and business network redesign, require commitment at the organisational level and, in particular, of senior managers. Throughout this book, we will aim to offer a range of these alternative approaches.

A note on terminology

The term 'e-business' is used as a generic concept to describe businesses that develop their organisational structure to 'fit' newer forms of information and communication technologies. This is not just about automating processes but about new kinds of services for, and relationships with, different users and stakeholders. Other terms currently abound in relation to a perceived e-revolution – e-commerce, e-procurement, e-access and e-care – to give just some examples. At the same time, these terms were already becoming out-of-date as the book was being written. IBM, for instance, coined the phrase 'on-demand business' in order to describe the underlying process change rather than the technologies that enable it (see Chapter 9). It is also proposed that we are moving towards a society where ICT is so ubiquitous that it ceases even to be an issue. New ICTs become so embedded we can always assume the availability of seamless (anytime, anyplace) access to, and integration of, services and information. However e-business is defined, the focus must be on adapting and transforming existing roles, structures and processes, and of using technologies to support this aim.

The structure of the book

The book is structured into two sections. First, we explore what can be learnt from e-business in redefining the relationships between enterprises and their users, and in developing changing processes to improve services, effectiveness and competitive advantage (Chapters 2–6). This section also examines how to provide an integrated and appropriate technology solution linked to business objectives. It looks at differences across the sector, and at the pros and cons of e-business for education. It aims to show how improving administrative efficiency, faster access and response to information, enhanced skills and knowledge development can actually lead to more high-quality face-to-face contact with students and a better student experience. Finally, this section explores the changing nature of educational services in the marketplace and the impact of private educational providers and global competition.

The second section (Chapters 7–9) looks at how post-compulsory education can get 'from here to there'. Initially it examines where the UK HE and FE sectors are now in terms of technological innovation and integration. It then looks in some detail at how to explore options and the kinds of leadership and vision required. It explores how risk assessment

and cost–benefit type analyses might be applied to post-compulsory education. It shows how educational institutions can map what already exists
and work towards redesigning organisational frameworks, relationships and
roles: altering where, when and how things happen. It suggests techniques
for overcoming barriers to change and successfully implementing improvements. Finally, it outlines the type of technologies required for an e-integrated
educational provision.

Towards managing education in an e-world

This book argues that it is time for higher and further education to look again
at how their businesses are managed, and to explore what can be learned
from the best of e-business practices. It examines what post-compulsory
education should be doing over the years ahead and how to manage the
organisational and technological changes required. It is not intended to
provide any kind of one-stop solution, or to underplay the complexities
and difficulties faced by HE and FE institutions in the UK. But it does insist
that these issues are urgent and relevant to the leaders and managers of
post-compulsory education.

Notes

1   For a different view see, for example, Scott Morton, M.S. (1991); Ernst, D.J.
    et al. (1994); and Dolence, M. and Norris, D. (1995); and also Michael Porter
    'Strategy and the Internet', *Harvard Business Review*, May 2001. Online.
    Available at www.sfu.ca/~anthonyc/cmpt301/301_case_files/pr/porter.pdf (ac-
    cessed 5 December 2006).
2   See, for example, Diana Laurillard (2002) and Steve Ryan *et al.* (2000).
3   See Paul McKey 'The Total Student Experience', NextEd Ltd for a good
    critique of conventional e-learning strategies from one of the new generation
    of commercial providers. Online. Available at www.nexted.com/nexted/white%
    2Dpapers/2/ (accessed 5 December 2006).

Bibliography

ACER and Cambridge Assessment (2006) Online. Available at www.unitest.org.uk/
    (accessed 5 December 2006).
Cunningham, J.L. and Hood, T.C. (1997) 'Public higher education and its consumers:
    ethical implications of multiple images of the university'. Online. Available at
    http://web.utk.edu/~unistudy/values/proc1997/jlc.htm (accessed 5 December 2006).
De Long, S. (1997–8) *As Long as its $Green: managing the sense-and-respond
    university for the 21st century*. Online. Available at http://hawk.fab2.albany.edu/
    $green/green.htm (accessed 5 December 2006).
Dolence, M. and Norris, D. (1995) 'Transforming higher education: a vision for
    learning in the information age', Society for College and University Planning.

Ernst, D.J., Katz, R.N. and Sack, J.R. (1994) 'Organisational and technological strategies for Higher Education in the Information Age', CAUSE Professional Papers Series No.13.

Gladwell, M. (2000) *The Tipping Point: how little things can make a big difference*, Boston, MA: Little Brown.

Goldstein, M. (2002) 'The economics of e-learning,' in *Teaching as E-business? Research and Policy Agendas*. Selected Conference Proceedings, Centre for Studies in Higher Education (CSHE), University of California, Berkeley. Paper CSHE3–0. Online. Available at http://repositories.cdlib.org/cshe/CSHE3–01 (accessed 5 December 2006).

Greenberg, M. (2004) 'A university is not a business (and other fantasies)'. *Education Review* March/April, Vol. 39, No (2). Online. Available at http://www.educause.edu/it/library/pdf/ERM0420.pdf (accessed 5 December 2006).

Johnstone, S. (2002) 'The complexity of decision-making', in *Teaching as E-business? Research and Policy Agendas*. Selected Conference Proceedings, Centre for Studies in Higher Education (CSHE), University of California, Berkeley. Online. Available at http://repositories.cdlib.org/cshe/CSHE3–01 (accessed 5 December 2006).

Laurillard, D. (2002) *Rethinking University Teaching*, 2nd ed. London: Routledge Falmer.

Matkin, G. (2002) 'Developing a conceptual framework and vocabulary for e-learning', in *Teaching as E-business? Research and Policy Agendas*. Selected Conference Proceedings, Centre for Studies in Higher Education (CSHE) University of California, Berkeley, October. Online. Available at http://repositories.cdlib.org/cshe/CSHE3–01 (accessed 5 December 2006).

Ryan, S., Scott, B., Freeman, H. and Patel, D. (2000) *The Virtual University: the Internet and resource-based learning*. London and Sterling, VA: Kogan Page.

Scott Morton, Michael S. (1991) *The Corporation of the 1990s: information technology and organizational transformation*. Oxford : Oxford University Press.

Chapter 2

The nature of an e-institution

Peter Ford

Universities and colleges in the UK and elsewhere are already developing new technologies for educational and administrative support. With the emergence of virtual and managed learning environments (VLEs and MLEs), online learning is being increasingly integrated with management information systems, with interoperability improving all the time. What, then, do best practices from e-business add to this? In what ways might an educational e-institution of the near future be noticeably different to existing provision?

The introductory chapter outlined how changing attitudes to our 'customers', new organisational roles and emerging technologies could shift the nature of post-compulsory education. This chapter expands on what forms of ICT are likely to have an impact and begins to imagine what university and college education might be like in an e-everything world; from the perspectives of students, teachers, researchers, administrators and senior managers.

The ubiquity of the Web: more of everything, everywhere

Over a very short period of time we have become very used to the Internet as a source of information via websites, and as a means of communication via email. Now, the growth in wireless networks with a new generation of broadband wireless technologies including WiMAX, is significantly increasing speed and connectivity while reducing cost. With the increase in business-to-business as well as business-to-consumer Web-enabled traffic, more robust and sophisticated systems and software are being designed that effectively handle many forms of online transactions and services. The Web has therefore moved from information to communication to exchange.

At the same time, in the move to digitisation more widely, familiar broadcast and telephone services are being outstripped by high-speed and cheap communications systems able to handle voice, pictures and all kinds of data easily. There are a growing number of personal devices (mobile phones, digital cameras, MP3 players, compact DVD players, digital TVs) that handle data in a variety of formats (XML, audio, streaming video, etc.). Together with the trend towards miniaturisation, there will be a new range of possibilities for truly portable information exchange. This is mass-customisation – allowing large numbers of people to have multimedia interaction with the precise services they need, whenever they need them.

Integration and collaboration: towards new forms of interactivity

Several trends point towards more integration and collaboration. For networks to be effective, they must be underpinned by both extending the sharing of resources and by common standards. Examples include:

- continuing support from developers for Open Source software;
- the adoption of Enterprise Systems;
- the easing of exchange processes through electronic data interchange (EDI);
- network advances, enabling the provision of wireless hotspots and local area networks (LANs), some with open access;
- an increasing number of social networking and sharing tools such as instant messaging, blogs, RSS, wikis, Flickr, Typepad;
- the extension of online gaming and virtual environments, such as Second Life, to education.

These new technologies don't just improve interoperability. They offer potentially new kinds of interactive 'spaces' and relationships with both data and other people.

Intelligent systems and software: pervasive computing

Rather than the simple exchange of information, emerging technologies focus on intelligent, responsive and directed support of human actions. New forms of searching and storage such as Blinkx or Dashboard act as search agents on behalf of their users, rather than just search systems. Similarly, new mechanisms such as global positioning systems (GPS), radio frequency identification devices (RFID), augmented and smart environments allow data to be manipulated both in time and space.

This is the growth of pervasive computing – context aware and self-learning automated systems based on the integration of mobile communications, ubiquitous embedded computer systems, consumer electronics and the power of the Internet. Devices communicate with other devices, sharing information and performing tasks without conscious human intervention. These devices are so embedded in the environment, and so natural to use, that they essentially become invisible to the user. During the next five to ten years, ubiquitous computing will come of age and the challenge of developing anywhere, anytime services will shift from demonstrating the basic concept to integrating it into the existing computing infrastructure and building innovative mass-scale applications that continue the computing evolution.

Towards the e-institution?

The argument from the best of e-business practices is that the effects of emerging technologies – Web ubiquity, mass-customisation, new forms of interactivity and pervasive computing – are about more than just a process of incremental addition to what we already know. How, then, would members of an e-institution of the near future experience post-compulsory education?

A student's perspective

The university or college card, a laptop and a mobile will be the heart of each student's study and social life. The cards enable cashless payments and access to places on campus; the laptop will be thin and light enough to carry anywhere, each coming with a college-designed standard desktop; in some institutions it will be provided free during the time of the student's study. The mobile will satisfy social needs, music, photography, games, SMS and video conversations: students will be able to opt to have college information by text, email or other media.

The whole campus will be wireless to allow access to the network anywhere; 24/7, with hot desks and charging stations distributed around the buildings. A docking station in students' rooms and other public places will provide links for laptop and mobile, and from these to speakers, charger, printer and projector.

The computer desktop will act as personal student portal providing customised access to networked software, tools, learning packages, knowledge repositories and other current information such as daily lecture lists, notes and notices. From it the student can make college-related financial transactions; update their personal information, select modules and class times and use library resources; keep in touch with friends; and access the institutional intranet for online exams, student feedback and personal development planning. They can personalise media preferences and are provided with an intelligent search agent which will learn from the choices they make.

For the early riser, attending lectures will continue to be an option. However, for latecomers the lecture appears on the screen, together with diagrams, and the lecture will be available to view and download from the Student Portal on demand. Cancellation of lectures (perhaps through lateness or unexpected bad weather) will be notified to the students through instant text messaging.

In between lectures there will be the sounds of rooms full of laptops being turned on or resumed, as everyone logs on, where relevant information and links are listed, including timetables and the email inbox. Perhaps the football team captain might email to notify everyone of a new kit collection at lunchtime. Logging on to the Account Section would reveal that the student's account had been debited. When the new kit arrives, the student takes some photos with their mobile phone, upload these wirelessly onto the laptop and email to parents and friends.

Canteen menus will also be electronic and updated in real time. Scanning the smart card will permit food selection and the canteen system will charge the appropriate amount to the account. Prior to an afternoon practical the student may choose a desk in a Quiet Docking Area and go through an online demonstration on the system to be used. This might be a quick video clip on the introduction of the new system, including a short test at the end to make sure the new terminologies have been understood.

In the evening there is the option to go through the day's new material, from the complete lecture notes now available on the laptop. Using Edit Mode, and while reading through the existing notes, the student's personal notes can be drawn up to improve understanding of the subject material, supported by intelligent searching of the Web. E-copies of most educational materials will be constantly accessible via a free digital repository. Remaining queries can be submitted to a chatroom session for the teacher to answer when available.

A teacher's perspective

The day would start by logging onto their own page on the staff Web portal. Course materials and activities for an introductory workshop would be downloaded. The system automatically selects the most appropriate printer and 3D prototyping machine for these, and then posts a message confirming they are ready for collection. These might be supplemented with practical activities and excerpts from online video demonstrations. Students will then be able to select and view later the ones they find most relevant to their own study development.

For teachers who are responsible for student entry to their subject area, the online profiler sofware will review incoming applications, set appropriate tests (including the submission of electronic portfolios) and make an indicative offer of level and modules, dependent on what length and mode of study the applicant has requested. Statistics, which are immediately updated to the desktop, will be monitored and a response given to those few applicants where the computer cannot make a clear decision.

This will eliminate the need to deal with everyone but, nevertheless, offer a clear picture of who is applying overall.

Instead of student entry being divided across admissions, enrolment and finance – and between administrative and academic staff – incoming students will deal with all of these through one portal, and both the departmental administrator and the teacher will have access to relevant data – thus enabling the feeding of the academic implications of student entry requirements into course management and development, while the administrator can monitor the financial and organisational implications for both the department and the institution.

A course development committee might then be presented with a case, based on demand shown in the student entry statistics, that there is a need to design a series of additional modules. Statistics will be easily gathered by the market intelligence unit, and employer and researcher representatives can support this through up-to-date market intelligence.

For the teaching itself, this might be prefaced by a message to the first-year students to remind them to bring their project work from the previous week and any other necessary prerequisites. This will appear both on mobiles and on laptops. The online learning environment could be accessed to track attendance and progress; noting perhaps that most have joined in the online discussions and downloaded materials. Some students may post messages that they are unwell and unable to attend. This information can be automatically sent to all the relevant people; other module tutors, the student's personal advisor and Student Academic Support. If a student is a persistent absentee, the system would initiate an alert to the personal advisor to check the situation, and to academic support to monitor implications for both students and courses.

When learning support colleagues meet for a briefing, the online system will flag up those students who are performing less well: the teaching staff can then agree how to work with those students. A learning support tutor might also take small groups throughout the morning to discuss relevant Web- and paper-based resources for their coursework. In groups students might prepare an electronic presentation on their work during the session. These could be broadcast in the refectory over lunch, so that everyone in the department can see work in progress, as well as being uploaded onto individual student webpages and course blogs.

Each student's record can be accessed on the system to see their previous studies, employment records, their progress log on this module, and all the tutorial notes to date. The next set of tasks can then be agreed and added to the online record.

At the end of the day the diary and calendar on the intranet will provide a reminder of events and deadlines. The downloadable forms for everything from travel expenses to course development proposal forms will be dealt with by an automated system which helps the teacher through the different processes. Forms no longer will be 'signed-off' by someone in authority. A travel claim would be submitted in the knowledge that the payment will be reimbursed directly to the teacher's account within days. Logging on to their own Continuing Professional Development (CPD) training area, a relevant day course can be identified which is available in two weeks' time. Signing up is immediate, and (constantly updating) rources in support available via a wiki.

A researcher's perspective

A researcher's life consists of obtaining grants, servicing previous grants, publishing results and submitting progress and final reports to the grant providers.

A research meeting may be required with colleagues in a different time zone. The Internet videoconference facility will allow for multiple connections, and an intensive dialogue using interactive whiteboards to explain ideas and to exchange material will prove low cost and effective. Document and moving-image transfer will be straightforward, and this will make such meetings highly productive. An outcome for all parties might be to agree to write a joint research proposal to a major multinational company, which would result in the exchange of all the necessary material required for the proposal to make it easy for the lead writer to put the whole document together. Details of costs, including salaries and overheads will be easily obtained from the local intranet and within hours a draft proposal can be circulated to colleagues across the world.

The system will alert the researcher to the need to submit an interim report on an existing research project funded, perhaps, by the European Commission. These alerts will be essential, since failure to submit the report on time can result in clawback of the funding. It will, however, be simple to look up the availability of research colleagues on the departmental electronic diary system and fix a meeting later in the day to decide how to proceed.

A trip abroad might need to be arranged for later in the month to make a research presentation of preliminary results and the travel budget is very tight. Searching for the lowest cost fare on the Internet, and booking it, together with prepaid airport parking, will take no more than a few minutes and is automatically charged to the departmental account.

A new research grant might become operative from the beginning of the following month and the required specialist computer systems might need to be ordered from the US. A quick trawl of the potential suppliers will yield prices, performance and availability. Reference sites for the most cost-effective options will be easily contacted and the necessary hardware and software can be quickly identified and ordered. Meetings with the head of department to obtain the necessary additional space within the department to site the equipment and the associated research students will prove easier than hitherto because of the online room-scheduling system, which quickly identifies the most cost-effective rearrangement of rooms and resources to accommodate needs.

An electronic scan of the day's offerings in the cafeteria might encourage an early lunch if the computer prediction is that the cafeteria will be very full within the hour. This will provide a backdrop for an afternoon of completing a research paper, to be published in one of the leading electronic journals in the field. Such a paper might be a compilation and enhancement from earlier conference proceedings, and incorporates interactive comments from other participants.

The rest of the day might be spent in the laboratory, talking to co-researchers and discussing how to solve some of the more pressing problems that the research projects have brought up. Advanced technologies will provide more time available each day for this essential part of a researcher's life, and the electronic aids, which shortened the administrative day, will prove invaluable.

Researchers work long and varied hours. On finally going home, a quick electronic call to the home computer will switch on the central heating, draw the curtains and recommend a recipe for dinner. Agreeing with its recommendations – it will have learned the preferences – by the time the researcher gets home it will be well advanced with preparation of the evening meal.

An administrator's perspective

The organisation of a major post-compulsory institution will involve a wide range of administrative processes covering planning, marketing, admissions, student progression, human resource management, estate management, and finance. All of these will be affected by embedded ICT. Data contained in staff, student and, in HE establishments, research databases will be combined to provide a powerful platform for comprehensive planning and monitoring.

Having agreed budgets at the beginning of the financial year, the finance officer will be able to rely on the system to provide alerts where there are potential budgetary over- or undershoots. It will then be possible to 'drill down' on the spending profiles and projections to determine the cause and issue revised forecasts. Projected out-turns relating to projects and individuals will allow tight financial monitoring and improved financial forecasting. Modelling a variety of scenarios (e.g. the introduction and distribution of top-up fees, cost of possible pay increases) will allow senior management to take informed decisions on the basis of up-to-date information which is obtained with the minimum of manual effort. Student billing and payment will be automated with online credit- and debit-card payment and debt management and recovery will be tightly monitored and thus made more efficient.

The academic administrator will be able to monitor adherence to quality procedures or academic targets through online analysis of progress on admissions, examiners' reports, staff-student committee minutes, and award classifications, while a comprehensive staff or student record will show details relating to any query over performance or personal circumstances. Communication with colleagues (both within and outside the institution) will be through electronic means such as email, texting and document transfer, while meeting schedules will be confirmed through electronic diarying. All staff will be required to ensure that their e-diaries are up-to-date.

The human-resource adviser will use the comprehensive staff record to register and monitor career development options, promotion criteria, sickness records, contracts of employment, study leave and holiday entitlement, and will be able to aggregate these records to provide planning data throughout the institution.

The estate manager will have comprehensive data on the estate as a planning tool. Data on buildings (heating, lighting, cleaning, maintenance costs, health and safety issues, refurbishment schedules) will be used for annual estate planning and budgeting. Online links to contractors for repair work will allow a fast response at a pre-negotiated cost. Online billing will feed directly into the finance system.

A senior management perspective

Senior management meetings focus on strategy and budget planning/ monitoring. Each member of the management team will have wireless connection to their chosen device which will have Internet and intranet access and support a wide variety of interrogation and modelling tools.

Consequent upon the discussion, up-to-date figures on student number projections; research grant income; budgets and income/expenditure forecasts will be immediately available, broken down on demand across a wide variety of departmental or functional headings for immediate analysis. New Web-based marketing materials can be scrutinised; estates planning and maintenance can be viewed and decisions can be taken and conveyed online to the relevant parties. Communications to departmental heads and external agencies can be agreed and actioned in real time.

Shared online diaries obviate the need for telephoning to identify availability for meetings; and comprehensive personnel records linking pay, conditions of employment, status and performance will be available for scrutiny and discussion when required. Issues raised by staff/students such as access and stocking of the library; performance of the IS infrastructure; speed of paying grants can be discussed with all the necessary data to hand.

Consequent upon strategic planning, the tools available will enable all managers to then individually manage their own portfolios using the appropriate levels of access allotted to them through the authentication system – which will permit access through one login to all authorised data and services; within the institution itself, to relevant stakeholders and to national facilities as appropriate.

A way forward?

Embedding ICT from an e-business perspective into the mainstream activities of an institution is likely to affect its nature, its mission, and its working practices. This chapter has attempted to paint a picture of aspects of such an institution. It should be emphasised that different educational establishments across HE and FE, and across the pre- and post-1992 universities in the UK, will have a variety of business drivers and a range of responses, based on what is relevant and achievable to them. Predictions are anyway notoriously unreliable. The intention here was not so much to aim for an accurate vision of the future as to stimulate ideas about how UK universities and colleges might be affected by emerging technologies, to challenge some current assumptions about how these institutions are run and the services they provide, and to imagine how education might change. The next three chapters – on what e-business is and how it might affect post-compulsory education – take this into further detail; and Chapters 6 to 9 explore how we might get 'from here to there'.

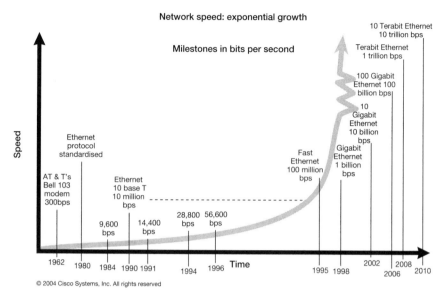

Figure 3.1 Diagram of rate change of networking technologies.

processes but developed new kinds of services for, and relationships with, their users. So what are the defining characteristics of such an organisation?

The shape of e-business

One of the main effects of technology has been to reduce the importance of the physical transfer of data, information or knowledge. Instead of an organisation having a 'fixed boundary' containing all its functions and services, these become potentially much more flexible across both space and time. This allows a virtual value chain to emerge whereby individuals from different locations, timeframes and organisations can work together efficiently and effectively. (What constitutes this virtual value chain in an educational context will be discussed in greater detail in the next chapter.) This affects not just the patterning of business processes within and between organisations, but also how business and customer relate to each other. E-businesses then, are not just businesses that provide online services to their customers (just as e-education as defined in this book is not just about virtual e-learning universities or colleges). They are organisations linked by networks and sharing applications and data, aiming to make significant reductions in costs and cycle times while also being able to improve customer service, quality and revenue.

Chapter 3

Learning from e-business

William Buller

There is no doubt that advances in information and communication technologies have been huge over the last few years and that they continue to accelerate. While Moore's law (1965) predicts a doubling of processing power every 18 months, similar advances are being made in storage costs and network speeds. One megabyte of storage now costs a few pence compared with nearly £50,000 fifty years ago when hard drives were invented. Network speeds are also growing exponentially. For instance 10 Gigabit Ethernet moves data at 10 billion bits per second, the equivalent of 73,529,412 people speaking at once.

But how have these advances actually changed the way we do business? Is it a question of faster chaos or have businesses been able to use technology to improve productivity? The impact of computer technology on business has been a talking point ever since Robert Solow stated in 1987, 'You can see the computer age everywhere but in the productivity statistics.' Since then, however, Alan Greenspan (US Federal Reserve Chairman) has spoken of *a remarkable run of economic growth that appears to have its roots in ongoing advances in technology* (1999). The Cisco-sponsored Net Impact Study conducted in 2003 estimated that about 48 per cent of the productivity gains between 1995 and 2003 were enabled by ICT investments (Momentum Research Group 2003). Recent work by the US Department of Labor produced a very similar estimate – technology accounted for 52 per cent of the productivity gains since 1948 (US Bureau of Labor Statistics).

Where might increases in productivity be found and what does a technology-enabled business look like? E-business is simply the application of technology to business processes to gain value and competitive/qualitative advantage. Where this process has been coherently and effectively applied it can have a significant impact on the way work is conducted; by cutting out inefficiencies and allowing tasks to be done faster, cheaper and more collaboratively. But this also means rethinking how a business is managed and about its relationships to customers, suppliers and other stakeholders. The rapid growth in companies such as Amazon and eBay are positive proof of the value of such thinking. They have not just automated their

Such networked virtual organisations have three main features:

Customer focus:
The ability to respond rapidly to customer demands by aligning the whole value chain around the customer so that they become central to the whole process rather than the recipient of the finished product or service.

Organisational integration:
Through the use of networked systems an organisation can link more closely to its customers, suppliers, partners and other members of the 'ecosystem' driving greater collaboration and allowing non-core activities to be outsourced.

Common systems:
Common networks and systems allow networked organisations to standardise processes and data, reducing the need for costly interfaces and enabling a seamless flow of information.

Transforming each of these areas has an impact on the experience of doing business for everyone involved (and is measurable through a number of important metrics such as output per head, cost-income ratios, customer satisfaction, cycle times and quality).

For example, by integrating customer data at all levels of the organisation, personalised customer requirements can be shared and addressed faster. Charles Schwab has used information technology and a network of outside financial advisors to create one of the world's most customer-centric organisations. Over the last decade the company has transformed itself from a discount broker with limited offerings to a full service financial services firm serving both institutional and individual customers. Much of this success has been due to the use of technology not just for online transaction processing but also to enable a unified customer repository. Whether a customer contacts the company in person at a branch, over the phone via a call centre or via the Web, all the relevant information is available in one place.

Many colleges and universities are moving towards a similar customer-centred approach through, for example, a 'one-stop shop' for recruitment and enrolment or a single portal for students to access educational and other services such as the payment of fees. But in most cases, these are at a relatively early stage, because the underlying organisational integration and implementation of common systems has not really happened.

Yet, increased effectiveness and significant savings of time and money should be the effects of adopting common standards across organisational networks, not only within an institution but also between it and other collaborators. This can enable closer integration with widely spread facilities

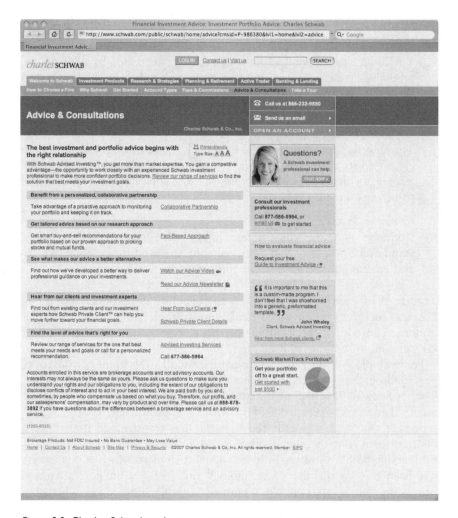

Figure 3.2 Charles Schwab website – a customer centric organisation.

and suppliers. Wal-Mart (which owns Asda in the UK), for example, has become the world's largest retailer due in large part to the sophisticated information network the firm has developed. This network links its suppliers directly with customer sales information from its thousands of stores. Retailers such as Wal-Mart have long been dependent on a network of companies to supply them with a wide variety of products carried in their stores. What Wal-Mart has done is to use its information technology to integrate these suppliers so tightly with its stores that the entire networked virtual ecosystem (NVE) operates as one entity. Their RetailLink programme uses an extranet to connect Wal-Mart buyers with over 10,000 suppliers and uses information from over 3,000 stores to analyse 10 million customer transactions each day.

Alternatively, it can enable institutions to define their special areas of excellence and to outsource non-central activities. Royal Philips Electronics is Europe's largest electronic company employing more than 180,000 people in 60 countries. This company recognised the need to focus on their core areas of design and marketing. Technology has allowed Philips to outsource manufacturing, testing, procurement and engineering to a partner. This has enabled them to improve efficiencies without losing control and responsiveness; with emerging technologies data sharing can be both robust and customised.

Cisco Systems are another example of how technology can drive real value at many levels. In the fiscal year to 2004, Cisco not only saved $2.2bn from the use of Internet Business Solutions but also increased customer satisfaction and market share. They leveraged additional value from all areas of the business; customer care, workforce optimisation, supply chain improvements and staff development/additional services via e-learning provision. Technology has impacted on processes across the business to such an extent that customer orders placed via the Web can be routed to outsourced manufacturers with the finished products being delivered to the customer without Cisco itself touching the actual product.

In addition, Cisco has innovated in the use of technology to drive efficiency in back office functions and uses its intranet to deliver employee services to all its 34,000 staff across the world. For example, Cisco employees can access HR and finance information online as well as a host of other employee and manager self-service applications covering recruitment, manpower planning, performance management, learning and development and multimedia communications regardless of location. In the process, the organisation was able to significantly reduce HR staff (as many functions have become 'self-service') with staff being able to alter relevant sections of their own records and make their own expenses claims (which are randomly monitored, rather than demanding individual signing off). Many aspects of HR and IT shared service centres have been made more efficient by supplementing them with Web-based FAQs and self-help tools to reduce the level of calls or to provide browse-with-me capability to improve effectiveness, while at the same time educating callers on best practice.

Cisco also builds in online educational support as an integral element of its employees' and customers' relationships. Technology provides staff with the ability to access online learning when they need it where they need it. Everyone can access, and add to, a knowledge repository, which helps build the whole organisation's knowledge and skills. In addition, news content can be distributed across the entire organisation very rapidly so that all training is up to date and available regardless of location. Most business organisations that use e-learning are incorporating it into their existing training programmes to supplement and replace expensive and time-consuming classroom instructor-led events. The result is a blended environment where assessment and knowledge transfer are often delivered using technology such as video on demand, virtual classrooms or Web-based multimedia delivery, leaving more time and money for skills development and coaching to be provided in a physical environment face to face. The benefits of e-business are not the sole prerogative of large global companies. Many small and medium enterprises have used e-business methods to make themselves more customer-centric. This has facilitated growth and profitability.

So, how can a post-compulsory educational institution learn from the core e-business characteristics of customer focus, organisational integration and common systems? Let's look at each of these in turn.

Customer focus – how technology supports e-business users

Much of the success high profile e-businesses (such as the ones outlined above) enjoy can be attributed to their focus on customers – not just as simple purchasers of products but as participants in a whole process. Amazon customers don't just browse and buy books, they add favourites lists and write reviews for other customers. They are not so much customers as 'members', able to provide immediate feedback both to the company and to other users of the service. The company is endlessly exploring new ways of adding value, such as customised book offers, related book lists, integrated new and second-hand services, the 'inside the book' feature and intelligent tracking of orders. Enabling customers to place orders online and to track the progress of these orders, as well as requesting and receiving support over the Web, puts them in control as well as speeding the entire process and reducing costs.

Many educational institutions are in the process of automating some or all of the transactions in support of a student's studies (such as paying fees, finding accommodation, selecting modules, ordering a book, claiming expenses or contracting visiting lecturers). New technologies are improving the security, integration, timeliness, accessibility and effectiveness of such support transactions, which can only enhance the student's total experience of the institution (as well as that of staff and other stakeholders). In addition, the student's experience of data is increasingly being integrated in universities and colleges via, for example, portals or single logins.

Emerging technologies (see Chapter 2) are also providing the ability to integrate all customer-facing channels (such as phone, Web, mail and face to face). This allows customers a choice of which communication mode they prefer; and enables all the resources of a business (whatever the origin

Figure 3.3 Amazon peer review and 'inside the book' features.

of text, voice or graphic message) to be integrated and interchangeable. Because they are connected across the network these resources can be in any office, any country or provided by any member of the integrated system. This environment is transparent to the customer who simply sees that they are getting a better service and that the individuals they come into contact with are integrated with one another.

At the same time, the best practices of e-business offer an approach to customer focus which is more than enabling a choice of channels or simply automating or integrating data. These companies are creatively exploiting what these new technologies can do to *re-define* the services they provide, focusing on the customer perspective. For example, British Airways provide online seat booking. Rather than the usual experience of queuing at an airport check-in desk and a seat being allocated by a clerk, the BA online system recognises your credit card to tell you which flight you are booked on, provides a seating plan from which you select your preferred location, and prints out a boarding pass. Control is passed from the seller to the buyer, making the process quicker and more responsive.

All HE and FE institutions in the UK already have a Web presence and an intranet. Many universities and colleges already undertake e-procurement, outsourcing, franchising or collaboration with external partners. But rather than these just being piecemeal and (usually) reactive developments, e-business aims to explicitly and systematically exploit *all* the locations where added value might be extracted from across all parts of the supply chain: by better managing stakeholder relationships; by improving the student experience; and by getting better value out of Web-enabled information and communication processes. This means both looking at where existing systems can be leveraged for increased benefit, and at where new processes and systems might enable large improvements.

To achieve this requires all staff that need it to have access to common systems holding customer and product information, to be able to share and collaborate with experts to resolve issues and to be able to complete transactions quickly and easily. Shared knowledge stores where individuals can search for solutions, contribute ideas and receive and provide feedback can reduce the time to resolve issues and improve quality. Communities of interest also allow people to get to know each other across long distances, to rate each other's work and build a virtual network of expertise and trust. The way that eBay and Amazon allow sellers/buyers and reviewers to rate each other against a set of shared and well-understood criteria is a simple and effective way of building trust and increasing value without large overheads.

Linking the objective of customer focus to the potential of Web-enabled networked technologies and systems also has an impact on post-compulsory education's core objective of teaching and learning. E-learning enables self-paced learning so students have more flexibility to focus on areas they have difficulty with, to fast track through a module, and to take learning when and where it is most convenient. An e-learning environment provides a rich form of content, linking external sources, video, simulations, gaming technologies, assessments and Web-based media that supplements the classroom and tutor environment. In addition, learning online makes collaboration, knowledge sharing and interaction with other students and moderators much easier as well as providing administrators with real time access to results and reports (see Chapter 5 for more discussion). At Cisco, for example, training is accessed via the Web, providing staff, customers and partners access to curricula, courseware, communities and support materials from any networked location. Entry, progression and achievement on demonstration of mastery rather than fixed amounts of time and study can offer multiple outcomes.

Customer focus, in the educational context then, means using technology to align all services around the student lifecycle, from marketing, application and entry through accommodation and pastoral care, curriculum management and assessment to career advice and the alumni programme. Portable electronic student records akin to National Insurance and health records (such as those being developed by the government through the Unique

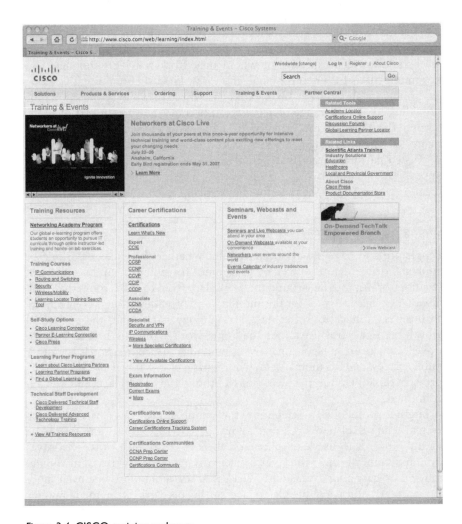

Figure 3.4 CISCO training webpage.

Learner Number and Signposter initiatives) are already enabling strategic initiatives around lifelong learning for UK universities and colleges.

Organisational Integration – changing business relationships and structures

An e-business has advantages over a traditional business because of the ways that it can interact with its integrated system of customers, partners, suppliers, employees and other stakeholders. By using the power of the Web to shrink distance and allowing physically remote people to respond as if they were in the next room, an e-business can operate more flexibly, faster and cheaper than an organisation relying on physical transfer of information and manual workflow. Technology means that people can enter data, access information and make decisions regardless of location and (with the correct level of security) irrespective of whom they work for. This shift has two key implications for organisational structures. First, the traditional working environment can be more flexible and cost-effective while at the same time providing for a wide range of activities. It becomes a different sort of place. Second, the impact of these trends is to remove the physical constraints from many activities allowing businesses to reorganise around extended networks of trusted partners rather than actual locations. Things happen in the most appropriate location (which may be entirely virtual), where the right person can do them at the right time for the right price.

Changing environments

People are and have always been mobile. Whether this means working or studying from remote offices or the home, travelling to and from work locations or just moving around the workplace from room to room there will always be a need to cater for this mobility and provide seamless connectivity to business applications and data. Technology is enabling the connected workforce in several ways. For the home worker there is broadband, for travellers there are hotspots (increasing in number in airports, hotels and other public places) and 3G mobile data, while wireless local area networks (LANs) provide flexibility for people to move about the workplace and remain connected.

Internet protocol (IP) Telephony, for example, provides a virtual phone system using data networks that allows people to log into any telephone in any office or to use a softphone on their PC to receive calls. This saves time and money both in the laying of networks (one not two) and in adding, moving or changing extensions. Wireless access points provide even more flexibility by allowing people to access the network with their systems and data without having to find a network connection. This means that connectivity can be provided in places where cables are inconvenient such as coffee bars, conference halls, retail outlets and workshops and flexible spaces that need to be reconfigured regularly.

In addition, the devices used to connect are proliferating from the PC to the mobile phone, tablet PC, kiosk or PDA hand-helds. These devices are much more likely to be personally owned and customised, with a fast cycle of updating and replacement.

At Glasgow Caledonian University, the Learning Café rethinks the old-style computer laboratory, in this context: providing students (and the public) with an Internet-style coffee bar containing a variety of ways to interact and connect, through a range of devices. This approach is being extended through a new-build learning centre that incorporates a range of new technologies such as RFID (radio frequency identification, allowing the electronic 'tagging' of objects or people) for locating books.

Figure 3.5 Glasgow Caledonian University Learning Café.

A fully integrated network does not just link people. It also links devices such as cameras, access points and building management systems (for lighting and heating) allowing these services to be interconnected and managed remotely; increasing flexibility, reducing costs and offering opportunities for additional revenue. In addition, by linking the security systems and access points to the corporate HR systems, new hires, temporary staff and leavers can have their access rights changed instantly.

In Birmingham, the Bullring retail centre has been fitted out with the latest technology to make it a SmartBuilding environment by Redstone Communications. This includes an end-to-end IP network for voice and video, and offers mobile connectivity delivering IP telephony and broadband services to all 132 retailers as well as the Bullring management team, plus more than 50 public hotspots. They also offer a wide variety of additional services including local data backup and virtual private network (VPN) linkage to corporate networks for security and closed-circuit TV. Advertising and sales promotion will also be done electronically across the network, reaching thousands of shoppers every day with multimedia advertising, sales promotions, job vacancies and other information on the numerous interactive touch-screens and plasma screens sited in the malls.

Changing organisational relationships

The second shift towards organisations being much more flexible is how they provide services across conventional functional or locational boundaries. The implications for education lie in the potential for high-quality shared services to be enabled across a campus, between campuses or throughout a network of colleges and schools. These services can be provided collaboratively or supplied by one partner that has chosen to specialise and can provide better, cheaper services than separate and individualised in-house provision. Or they can be outsourced to an external business. For example, private organisations already provide and support the personal development plan (PDP) process for many American universities and colleges, sharing data on students through Web-enabled networks without threatening security, and linking that data to wider systems of career and employment advice.

Systematic integration of this sort allows educational organisations to focus on their core skill areas such as research, curriculum management, teaching and marketing while partnering on non-core activities such as facilities management, accommodation, finance and administration; and to do this without losing data control or security. This enables valuable economies of scale and helps institutions concentrate on, and become, centres of excellence in their specialised areas, rather than dissipating their energies across a disparate range of historically accumulated activities.

However, although it has become common practice to outsource more generic services such as cleaning and maintenance, universities and colleges remain relatively unadventurous in other forms of sharing and delegating. This, of course, has been most highly resisted in terms of sharing educational materials, not just in terms of specific 'chunks' of e-learning, but also at the level of franchising entire courses.

Technology has a significant impact on the way businesses are organised but it also has an effect on the way individuals work. Not only does it free them up to work anywhere but it allows them to collaborate more effectively with each other, to learn knowledge and skills for their job more conveniently and to work as part of an integrated team rather than isolated individuals. By supporting process automation with transparent workflow and personalised alerts, organisations can let their people focus on doing what is important without having to spend time worrying about chasing documents or re-entering data.

This use of technology increases the time that people can spend working with others to deliver value. Whether this is with suppliers, customers, partners or students, the great advantage that technology brings is to add flexibility so that people can have the knowledge, learning, tools and expertise where they need it, when they need it. This is as relevant for a university or college as it is for a manufacturer or retailer. Where resources are scarce – as they are in post-compulsory education – it makes sense to use the power of new technologies to integrate and improve support systems so as to enable tutors and other learning support staff to do what they do best, that is, work face to face with students.

Common systems – standardisation of common processes, data and technology

Underpinning the major changes in the way an e-business interacts with its customers and with a wider integrated system is a complex structure of applications, data and networks potentially connecting everyone to everything. For this to be effective and drive value there needs to be seamless communication without manual intervention or the need for costly enhancements. This means standardisation of process, application and data wherever possible and appropriate. There are two key elements to this standardisation – common business processes and data, and a standards-based integrated ICT infrastructure.

Common business processes and data

One of the problems most organisations face when launching an e-business strategy is that their internal processes are poorly organised. Instead of having just one way of handling sales or recruitment, a company might have a different process for each division or location. Each of these divisions might also have its own set of customer and product data even though they may share both. Having different ways of handling orders and multiple sets of customer data makes fully automating the process, let alone integrating it with partners, next to impossible. Most post-compulsory educational institutions will recognise these sorts of difficulties.

Organisations must first create a standard way of performing key business processes using a standard set of data. This then paves the way for implementing end to end processes across the business functions – such as 'Quote to Cash', which links sales, operations, marketing, manufacturing and finance into a single process aimed at moving from the point of customer interest through delivery of service and collection of cash seamlessly using linked applications and a single source of customer data.

Many organisations continue to suffer from the duplications and gaps of non-common systems. Many post-compulsory institutions are using portal technology to enable some degree of interoperability. However, it is only in rethinking how to improve the underlying operational business processes themselves, that the potential of common systems can be fully realised.

Standard ICT infrastructure

In addition to standard processes and data it is essential to support these with a standard ICT infrastructure that operates in real time. This allows decisions to be taken faster with more information than before and for executives to monitor total business performance at a high level so as to be able to drill down to specific items and get detailed information as required.

Open standards are the first step to success. Communications, data exchange and the linking of applications are possible only if different organisations have agreed on a common set of data and technology standards in addition to shared processes. Technology vendors have appreciated this and provided development and support for standard protocols and technologies such as Shareable Content Object Reference Model (SCORM), Extensible Mark-up Language (XML), Simple Object Access Protocol (SOAP) and Internet Protocol (IP). This is in part due to the success of the Internet whose standards-based architecture has opened up a whole new realm of collaboration and cross enterprise working. What HTML (a common mark-up language) and HTTP (a common protocol for sharing information) did for the Web, XML and Web services protocols such as SOAP will do for data exchange and application-to-application communication. Developments in the design of managed learning environments (MLEs) are tending to take a similar, open standards–open source (sharable programming) approach.[1]

There are three main layers to a shared architecture that need to be considered:

1   foundation technology – This includes the physical infrastructure of networks, access devices, security and entitlement and content management. It is essential for this layer to be integrated and connected if people, applications and devices that use it are going to interact.

2   enabling technologies – This layer includes data repositories and transaction systems covering areas such as HR, finance, customers and knowledge. These handle the basic data that businesses use to conduct operations as well as providing the core software environment in which user-facing applications operate.

3   networked applications – This layer includes business and user-facing applications that run on the network to provide functionality to everyone in the organisation and an integrated system. These applications are often Web-based and simple allowing rapid and cost effective development and deployment as well as providing a host of services including calculations, quotes, workflow, reporting and data entry.

This architecture provides a high degree of flexibility and personalisation for the user while using the underlying network and data to deliver scalability and power. For example, there may be several groups who wish to view and, in some cases, update student records. This could include students registering interest in a course, institutions providing references, tutors updating assessment records and employees browsing CVs. This architecture allows each of these groups to access the same core data but provides personalisation, user friendliness and ensures confidentiality in relation to each different process.

It also means that an organisation can clarify which common processes must be implemented to allow effective cross-integration and customer focus and where there is room for localised and autonomous processes and systems.

Conclusion

Learning from e-business is not about 'being told' that the way forward for post-compulsory education is by becoming virtual or e-learning-based institutions. Universities and colleges are developing a wide variety of hybrid models from entirely distant learning to entirely face-to-face educational services. All can learn from the best practices of e-business. Nor does it mean that education has to become more like an entirely profit-oriented business. Universities and colleges rightly define their own aims and objectives across economic, social and academic concerns. But, in deciding how to improve educational services for the post-compulsory sector – whether face-to-face, online or hybrid – e-business can offer some interesting ideas and approaches about making better relationships between organisations and their users, so as to best exploit emerging technologies.

This raises two questions. First, just what sort of e-business is post-compulsory education? Where does it have similarities or analogous processes to an e-business model and where is it a distinctly different sort of entity? Second, how can we develop the issues covered by this chapter so as to see where – across the whole range of its academic and administrative processes – post-compulsory education can learn lessons from the best of e-business practices? These are questions considered in Chapter 4.

Note

1   For example, see the JISC MLE toolkit (MLE design and technology options). Online. Available at www.jiscinfonet.ac.uk/InfoKits/creating-an-mle/mle-design/index_html.

Bibliography

Greenspan, A. (1999) 'Before the Joint Economic Committee', US Congress, 14 June. Online. Available at www.federalreserve.gov/boarddocs/Testimony/1999/19990614.htm (accessed 12 December 2006).

Momentum Research Group (2003) 'Net impact study'. Online. Available at www.momentumresearchgroup.com/reports.html (accessed 12 December 2006).

Moore, G. (1965) 'Moores Law', *Electronics* 19 April, 38(8). Online. Available at ftp://download.intel.com/museum/Moores_Law/Articles-Press_Releases/Gordon_Moore_1965_Article.pdf (accessed 12 December 2006).

Solow, R. (1987) 'You can see the computer age everywhere but in the productivity statistics'. *New York Review of Books* 12 July.

Chapter 4

What sort of e-business is post-compulsory education?

John Powell

As suggested in Chapter 1, the divide between 'business' and 'education' is blurring. This blurring is part of a larger transformation of the public sector, under pressure from governments to deliver 'efficiency' and cost savings. The assumption that market- or profit-driven organisations will be more effective in these regards has underpinned both the privatisation and the 'marketisation' of erstwhile public sector activities – for instance healthcare. Education, and especially post-compulsory education, has been pursuing such a path (often reluctantly) for more than a decade in the UK. This is being driven partly by the developing competition for students (and for other sources of revenue) between universities and colleges in the UK and globally. It is also the consequence of the increasing significance of the private sector in the management and provision of educational services, both as a consequence of explicit government policy and as a result of rising corporate and other private sector provision of 'educational services'. The impact of some of these issues is explored in greater detail in Chapters 5 and 6. In this chapter we will explore specifically what kind of e-business models might be appropriate to post-compulsory education, and how this helps open up our thinking about its provision in an e-revolution.

As Arthur Levine argues, a number of forces are driving privatisation, particularly in higher education. Perhaps the most significant is:

> the rise of an information-based economy. Now the sources of wealth come from knowledge and communication instead of natural resources and physical labor . . . This is a global rather than a national economy. The New Economy puts a premium on intellectual capital and the people who produce it. This means that the demand for higher education is expanding dramatically. Education is needed throughout a lifetime, and the marketplace for that education is international. This growth makes education appealing to the private sector.
>
> (Levine 2000: 1)

Pragmatically, institutions are learning from, and adapting to, such changes in environment. How, then, can the management tools and concepts applied to e-businesses be used within education? The aim of this chapter is to utilise the analytical frameworks that have been applied to e-business and map them to post-compulsory education. It builds on the fundamentals of networked virtual organisations identified in Chapter 3 – customer focus, organisational integration and common systems – but also explores the background context of e-business in relation to post-compulsory education.

Education and the market

There are a number of education-specific issues, particularly in relation to market transactions, are not easily resolved or that may necessitate further debate and discussion. In part, one purpose of this chapter is to stimulate constructive discussions about the relationships between education and business. An interest in e-business practices can suggest that post-compulsory education can or should be addressed as a business. Notwithstanding the privatisation pressures noted above, we need to look at the complications of treating education as a business. Here, we will start by looking at two of these problems: first, the nature of the educational marketplace and second, the conflation of customer and student.

If we are defining a market then, in very simple terms, 'a market exists whenever buyers and sellers exchange goods or services – usually for money' (Lipsey and Chrystal 2004: 39). The typical economist's expectation is that the interaction of buyers and sellers within the market will produce a quantity of transactions agreed at a particular price. The relationship between supply (the quantity of the goods or services sellers are willing to sell) and demand (the quantity the buyers wish to purchase) is mediated by price. Higher prices, for instance, will tend to ration demand. There are, naturally, greater complexities that can be added but the fundamental principles still underpin them – namely, that both buyers and sellers are motivated by self-interest. This is manifested as a desire to generate profit by sellers (the profit motive, which we ascribe to 'business') and a desire to produce satisfaction through consumption by buyers ('consumers'). These interests push sellers and buyers in opposite directions but, to restate, this is mediated by the market, through price.

To apply these basic concepts to post-compulsory education in countries such as the UK might initially appear straightforward. The sellers, in our application, are educational institutions offering educational services and the like for exchange. Buyers are potential students seeking educational services. However, it is at this point that our simple economic modelling of the market-place runs into some difficulties. How is price determined in this market? For the majority of UK HE institutions, for instance, in a pre-tuition fees environment, price was not set by the interaction of demand and supply because there was no 'price' as such (in the sense of what buyers paid for the service). Institutions received funding per student from local authorities (which pre-1992 may have had ownership of the institution, in the case of the polytechnics). As tuition fees have been introduced in England, a price label may perhaps be attached to tuition fees (though there are complications here, too). For 2006 undergraduate entry, for example, the English HE environment had so-called variable fees. However, the fee's maximum ceiling had been pre-set by the government and the majority of institutions had gone for the maximum level. Where variations occur, it is in the level of bursaries and/or grants on offer to students. The basic outcome is that if this is a market in the traditional sense, it is one that has had substantial intervention by the state. Consequently, there is no 'market mechanism' in operation, no balancing of demand and supply by price. Although there may be sound social reasons to welcome this, it means that the 'market' does not work like a market in practice.

Economists have also traditionally described education as a 'merit good' – that is, a good that if provided solely by the market would be under-consumed, both in terms of the benefits of such consumption to the individual and to society as a whole (healthcare is similarly categorised). In the past, this has been the motive for state provision of education. However, as noted earlier, there are pressures in the UK and elsewhere that have pushed 'marketisation' into the public sector. Most post-compulsory educational institutions have not, traditionally, been profit-driven organisations, emerging as they have from the public sector and a public service orientation. That is not to say that institutions have not made this reorientation, but that often the culture of many organisations has not historically supported a profit-driven ethos. However, a concern with cost reduction and efficiency has become more evident within many institutions and most would regard, for instance, the undergraduate recruitment environment as 'competitive' (although, as noted above, this does not typically reflect price competition).

How do we define the buyers of education services, though? The initial reaction might be to say that students are the buyers, as they are obviously the immediate beneficiaries of the educational services proffered by sellers. However, it is perhaps not that clear. For instance, in HE under the UK's variable fees for 2006 entry, the students starting at universities and colleges did not have to pay up-front for the educational services received (unless they explicitly chose to do so). Effectively, the state is paying initially and graduates will eventually incur a graduate tax from their salaries to recoup the tuition fees paid to the institutions. So, students are buying educational services, and consuming educational services, but not immediately paying for those educational services. Can we still consider them to be 'buyers' on this basis? Probably, but this dimension does confuse the issue somewhat. It may be simpler to consider students as 'consumers' first, and not necessarily buyers. This would still make them 'customers', but we still need to be mindful of the other aspects of the student–institution relationship.

Finally, and perhaps most obviously, not all potential 'consumers' become students. They must first apply and be accepted. Some are not allowed to 'buy' post-compulsory educational services or can only do so when they have met conditions set by the 'seller'.

If we were to imagine how a 'true' market might impinge on the provision of educational services we can perhaps see how far this still is from the current state of much post-compulsory education (or perhaps how close it is). Under our imagined market, students would bid for educational services (and institutions would be competing with each other to attract the 'best' customers). At an institutional level, the price of a particular qualification might be determined by the demand for that course. Less attractive courses would be cheap (to attract students) or not offered at all by institutions. Courses with high levels of demand would be able to charge premium prices, backed up by the brand of the institution. Even at an individual module level one might expect to see differential pricing in operation and perhaps even different levels of service on offer – a lower price for a non-attendance mode, with additional fees for lectures, for tutorials, for having feedback on coursework, access fees for having discussions with tutors. Similarly, more popular members of staff may be able to charge students more than less popular ones (and how much of this revenue do individual members of staff get to retain, as incentive perhaps?). All potential students could buy academic services somewhere, at some price, whatever their current qualifications. Some institutions might only collect fees on the basis of successful completion (a no win, no fees model). Arguably, we are a long way from this kind of educational market. Nonetheless, some (like Levine 2000) would argue that the future holds some of these outcomes as education is increasingly privatised. The National Education Association's *Future of Higher Education*, excerpted on the NEA website[1] offers a fuller exploration of such a market-driven future. One small example of this more market-driven view would be the University of Phoenix MBA. It has 40,000 students a year taken on weekly on a rolling programme, meeting a demand for start date flexibility while keeping class sizes to an average of fifteen.

Education as an intangible service

In the introduction to this book (chapter 1), it was suggested that the fundamental concerns of post-compulsory education could be simplistically summarised as the provision of educational services, the granting of awards for educational achievement and the development of academic subject knowledge. These, in turn, might be elaborated as a more detailed set of processes (which will have different drivers, priorities and organisational structures for different educational institutions) – for example: attracting, retaining and progressing students; creating and updating educational content; providing teaching and learning services; providing student support;

educational processes management; resource management; staff support and management; accreditation services; quality assurance; creating intellectual property rights; research; consultancy services and so on.

Each of these activities is reflective of the 'information-based economy', as Levine (2000: 1) put it. Education is a service or an intangible product. If we focus on the first activity – the provision of educational services – then we may also view the 'output' from universities and colleges (students, graduates) as consumers of an 'experience good'. Experience goods (Nelson 1970) are products or services whose characteristics cannot be determined before consumption. From an e-business perspective, Choi et al.(1997) propose a framework for considering digital products that defines intangibles in the context of three dimensions – the nature of the product/service, the delivery agent used to provide the product/service and the underpinning process. The broad division along each of these dimensions is between physical and digital (or virtual). The framework maps a number of possible combinations of product, delivery agent and process, in physical and virtual terms. As a framework, Choi et al.'s work can help us to define some boundaries for educational services, in an e-business context (see Figure 4.1).

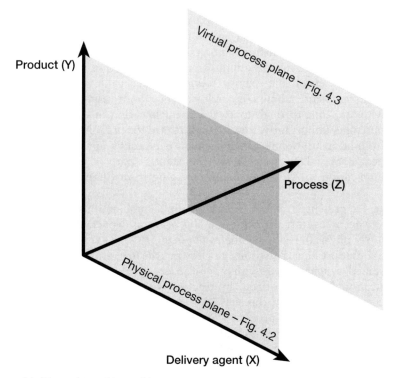

Figure 4.1 Dimensions of intangibles.
Source: adapted from Choi et al. 1997.

As far as post-secondary education is concerned, let us align the three dimensions as follows (see Figures 4.2 and 4.3):

Product/service (Y dimension):
This represents the education experience good. In itself it is intangible – a service – but the provision of the service, including where and how the service is provided may be *physical*, in the sense of a classroom or other learning environment and may be experienced with other learners, or *virtual* (experienced and mediated online).

Delivery agent (X dimension):
In this case, we are talking about *how* the educational service is delivered, which also implies *by whom* it is delivered. Again, the dimensions are *physical*, in the sense of the teaching staff being either physically present with learners or *virtually* present, with the online environment acting as delivery mechanism (either directly or indirectly intermediating between students and teaching staff).

Process (Z dimension):
Choi *et al.* were predominantly concerned with process in the sense of a *delivery* process, distinguishing between delivered products and interactive products. In an education context, however, we can take process as being something more fundamental. Let us regard *process* as akin to the administrative processes necessary to provide educational services – effectively the administrative infrastructure, from recruitment processes, enrolment, paying fees, managing academic activities such as assignment submission and student progression, communication with students, through to award of qualification or other educational outcome. Importantly, this does not regard the organisational processes from an institutional or management perspective but from the student perspective. This in itself is a substantial part of the management implications of customer focus, emerging from Chapter 3.

Figure 4.2 presents a matrix of four possible combinations of product and delivery agent, against a background of *process* (as defined above) remaining resolutely physical. Cell 1 combines *physical product* – educational services offered within the classroom or lecture theatre and, by implication, 'consumed' synchronously with other learners – with *physical delivery agent* – educational services offered by teaching staff physically present within the class. Underpinning this cell (and the others in Figure 4.2 too) is a physical administrative process. If we return to the adaptation of Matkin's (2002) educational strategies and services outlined in Chapter 1, cell 1 in the matrix clearly represents **traditional learning**.

Cell 4 in Figure 4.2, on the other hand, combines virtual product and virtual delivery agent (but with a physical administrative process). In Matkin's typology, then, this cell would represent **distance learning**.

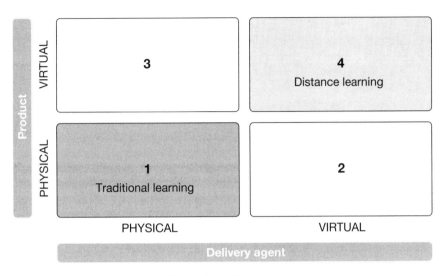

Figure 4.2 Dimensions of intangibles – physical process plane.
Source: adapted from Choi *et al.* 1997.

The adaptation of Matkin in Chapter 1 offers two further points on the spectrum between traditional and distance learning that we can map within the matrix. *Blended learning* (which supplements face-to-face learning with online materials) might combine cell 1 with cell 2, adding an element of virtual delivery agent to the physical process. *Hybrid learning* (which combines online learning with classroom study) might combine cell 3 with cell 1. Figure 4.2, therefore, allows us map the range of e-learning opportunities an institution may pursue.

Figure 4.2's combinations, however, are built on purely physical administrative processes. If we move from physical to virtual administration processes, as shown in Figure 4.3, then substantial depth is added to the e-business opportunities that educational institutions can pursue. The four educational strategies map to similar quadrants in Figure 4.3 as they did in Figure 4.2 (as we have not changed the X and Y dimensions of delivery agent and product). However, the *implications* of that mapping are substantially different.

In Choi *et al.*'s original conception, the equivalent of cell 8 in Figure 4.3 represents the 'core' of e-business – the 'pure play' of virtual product, virtual delivery agent and, importantly, virtual process. In our educational application, distance education is moved to a fully virtual, online-enabled experience. The outcome for the other modes of Matkin's educational strategies is that they become similarly underpinned by a set of customer-focused online administrative processes.

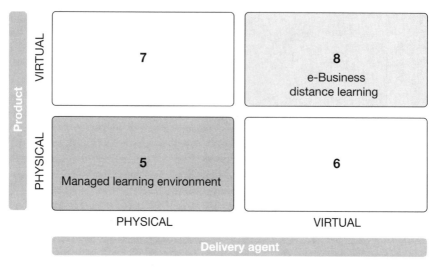

Figure 4.3 Dimensions of intangibles – virtual process plane.
Source: adapted from Choi *et al.* 1997.

Although e-learning strategies may reflect a more visible part of education's adaptation to the information economy, the administrative infrastructure of educational institutions – the process dimension – is where fundamental responses to the growth of e-business have already taken place (see for instance NOIE's (2002) 'e-business in Education'). We will next examine some of the potential scope that is offered by e-business to what Michael Porter (1985) terms support activities and primary activities.

The value chain

In the context of the management tool that frames this book – the MIT 90s model – Michael Porter's value chain is an important foundation for the focus on 'business process' that the MIT 90s model adopts (Coombs and Hull 1997). Fingar *et al.* note that 'e-commerce provides the business platform for realising Porter's visions' (1999: 2).

The value chain divides an organisation into primary and support activities. Porter argues that the value chain is the "basic tool for under-standing the influence of information technology on companies (Porter 2001: 74). As Mintzberg *et al.* explain, the basic division in the value chain is between primary and secondary activities:

> **Primary activities** are directly involved in the flow of product to the customer, and include inbound logistics (receiving, storing, etc.),

operations (or transformation), outbound logistics (order processing, physical distribution, etc.), marketing and sales, and service (installation, repair, etc.). **Support activities** exist to support primary activities. They include procurement, technology development, human resource management, and provision of the firm's infrastructure (including finance, accounting, general management, etc.). [see Figure 4.4]

(1998: 104)

Support activities are associated both with particular primary activities and with the value chain as a whole (with the exception of firm infrastructure, which 'oversees' the entire value chain). At each stage of the value chain, as one moves through the different primary activities, the firm will be seeking to maintain or improve its profit margins (in terms of the base cost of undertaking the activity versus the revenue that activity generates). Within an industry, there may be a whole series of interlinked value chains, representing the entire supply chain from raw material to final consumer.

There are a number of observations we can make in mapping the value chain concept to post-compulsory education. For a typical business, the first three primary activities – inbound logistics, operations, outbound logistics – comprise the supply chain (and thus the focus of supply chain management, with the fundamental tie-in to procurement). By supply chain, we mean the relationship between the firm's suppliers (for a manufacturer, of components and raw materials, say) and the firm's transformation process enacted upon those inputs to produce the good that the firm will sell its customers and ship out via outbound logistics. For education (and for many

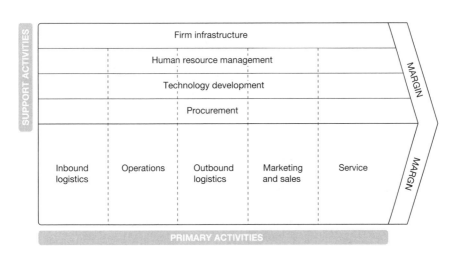

Figure 4.4 Porter's generic value chain.

Source: Mintzberg *et al.* 1998 from Porter 1985.

other intangible services), however, the supply chain may not really be a major part of primary activities. Again, if we refer back to the 'core business' of education as identified previously – the provision of educational services, the granting of awards for educational achievement and the development of academic subject knowledge – the key focus is 'operations'; that is, effectively the provision of academic services. We might also wonder about outbound logistics in the context of post-secondary education. Do we mean successful completion and award of qualifications, for instance? Would graduation ceremonies be HE or FE's outbound logistics?

A more significant fit with education is that of marketing and sales (along with service) activities. When combined with the ongoing 'service provision' of operations, this set of activities effectively defines the organisational scope of customer relationship management (CRM). As we have already noted, this reflects one of the fundamental characteristic of e-business – customer focus. To return to the adaptation of Choi *et al.*'s dimensions of intangibles approach discussed above (see Figures 4.1–4.3), Porter's primary activities for education can be mapped to the product/service (Y) and delivery agent (X) dimensions. Support activities can be mapped to the process dimension (Z). The most relevant aspects of the value chain to post-compulsory education may therefore be the explicit identification of what constitutes Porter's 'secondary' or support activities.

We have already recognised that, in practical terms, one of the most significant impacts of e-business on education is already being felt in administrative processes. Porter's exploration of the impact of e-business practices on support activities in his HBR article, 'Strategy and the Internet', notes that:

> Because every activity involves the creation, processing and communication of information, information technology has a pervasive influence on the value chain. The special advantage of the Internet is the ability to link one activity with others and make real-time data created in one activity widely available, both within the company and with outside suppliers, channels and customers.
>
> (2001: 74)

The opportunities for educational institutions afforded by e-business practices are in many ways, therefore, very similar to those for business, as identified by Porter. Thus, he notes several applications of the Internet to support activities that have direct relevance to support activities in education (i.e. process dimension activities), including:

Firm Infrastructure
- Web-based, distributed financial and enterprise resource planning (ERP) systems.

Human Resource Management
- self-service personnel and benefits administration;
- Web-based training;
- Internet-based sharing and dissemination of company information;
- electronic time and expense reporting.

Procurement
- linkage of purchase, inventory and forecasting systems with suppliers;
- direct and indirect procurement via marketplaces, exchanges, auctions and buyer-seller matching.

(Porter 2001: 75)

At the same time, this needs to be exposed as more than the simple automation or 'webification' of these processes. Levine has argued that there are several likely consequences of the privatisation of education. There are two particular concerns that are relevant in exploring the application of the value chain framework. The first of these is the 'unbundling of the traditional functions of higher education' (Levine 2000: 5). The second, revealed through this reworking of the Porter value chain in an educational, Web-enabled context, is the importance of the process dimension.

Unbundling education?

'Unbundling' can also be described as the 'deconstruction of the value chain', where the traditionally integrated process of production or service provision becomes increasingly fragmented, with multiple firms providing (ever smaller) parts of the overall process. Jelassi and Enders cite the example of the PC industry during the 1990s, which became increasingly fragmented in terms of the number of firms involved at each stage in the *overall* industry value chain, comprising components (processors, memory, etc.), PCs, OSs, application software and marketing and distribution (Jelassi and Enders 2005: 155). Levine asserts that, of the core activities in education (which he identifies as teaching, research and services), only teaching is universally profitable. Research, he suggests, is only profitable to a small minority of institutions. 'Unbundling', for Levine, implies that competition will emerge within the teaching area which, when combined with the individualisation of HE (the outcome of an anytime, anyplace access to educational services), will result in a deconstruction of the traditional education value chain (Levine, 2000: 5).

Institutions will have to embrace such changes, both at the process level (Porter's support activities) and in terms of the relationship between the institution and students, covering both service and process. As suggested by Burnett and Oblinger:

Several lessons have emerged from our best practice institutions. First and foremost is focus: services are shifting from student interactions focusing solely on 'transactions' to student interactions concerned with the 'customer experience' and building lifelong relationships.

(2002: v)

Burnett and Oblinger have characterised such best practice as 'high touch/ high tech', with information technology underpinning the student-institution relationship, in both service and process terms. We will be returning to the theme of 'unbundling' through later chapters in this book, particularly chapter 5.

Next, though, we turn to examining the importance of the process dimensions.

E-business models and education processes

As Pateli and Giaglis note, in an article analysing e-business models:

the accelerating growth of e-Business has raised the interest in transforming traditional business models or developing new ones that better exploit the opportunities enabled by technological innovations.

(2004: 302)

One of the consequences of the discussion above, on education as an intangible, is the significance of *process* as far as e-business opportunities in education are concerned. To further explore these we must examine relevant e-business models. Michael Rappa (2005) offers a broad outline of what we mean when we talk about business models:

In the most basic sense, a business model is the method of doing business by which a company can sustain itself – that is, generate revenue. The business model spells out how a company makes money by specifying where it is positioned in the value chain.

This requires some clarity about the extent to which post-compulsory education is revenue generating (an issue already raised implicitly when examining the extent to which markets exist in education). It also needs some understanding of the range of possible e-business models, so as to determine whether post-compulsory education fits any of the existing perspectives. Finally, we will also need to explore some of the business concepts implied above, such as Porter's value chain.

There have been many debates as to whether the Web and new technologies have enabled new kinds of business models, or merely variations on conventional approaches. The literature review by Osterwalder and Pigneur suggests that there are a number of reasons why the understanding and use of e-business models in particular is necessary, including: allowing managers to develop their own understanding 'of relevant elements' and to 'communicate and share understanding . . . among other stakeholders' (Osterwalder and Pigneur 2002: 2), facilitating change, identifying measures with which to assess performance and allowing managers to simulate and learn about e-businesses. These benefits apply equally to managers within post-compulsory education who are seeking to develop and apply e-business techniques to education.

Michael Rappa identifies nine categories or types of e-business model, listed below, and which are explained in greater detail on his digital enterprises site (Rappa 2005):

1   brokerage;
2   advertising;
3   infomediary;
4   merchant;
5   manufacturer (direct);
6   affiliate;
7   community;
8   subscription;
9   utility.

From this set, only three categories have some direct relevance to post-compulsory education in that they relate to experience goods and to some element of public service – the direct model, the community model and the subscription model. These are summarised below:

Direct model

> The . . . 'direct model' . . . is predicated on the power of the Web to allow . . . a company that creates a product or service . . . to reach buyers directly and thereby compress the distribution channel. The . . . model can be based on efficiency, improved customer service, and a better understanding of customer preferences.
>
> (Rappa 2005)

In the context of post-compulsory education, the *direct* aspect of this model on the Web would reflect cell 8 in Figure 4.3; that is, the 'pure play' of distance education – virtual product, virtual delivery agent and virtual process. Fee-based education will clearly deliver revenue in this context.

Community model

> The viability of the community model is based on user loyalty. Users have a high investment in both time and emotion. Revenue can be

based on the sale of ancillary products and services or voluntary contributions; or revenue may be tied to contextual advertising and subscriptions for premium services. The Internet is inherently suited to community business models and today this is one of the more fertile areas of development, as seen in rise of social networking.

(Rappa 2005)

Rappa identifies open source software, public broadcasting and knowledge networks as examples of the community model. In the context of post-compulsory education, the community aspect reflects the community of students, both as an identifiable body of users of the education services of a particular institution (and perhaps in general as well) and as a community with other common interests that are not tied to education but to other demographic or social aspects. Generating revenue from a community model will be driven by the sale of products and services to the student body, over and above the provision of 'basic' educational services.

Subscription model

Users are charged a periodic – daily, monthly or annual – fee to subscribe to a service. It is not uncommon for sites to combine free content with 'premium' (i.e., subscriber- or member-only) content. Subscription fees are incurred irrespective of actual usage rates.'

(Rappa 2005)

The examples Rappa suggests for the subscription model include content providers like Netflix, person-to-person networking services (such as Friends Reunited) and ISPs. The fee-based HE environment has produced similarities to the subscription model, although students could, of course, be seen as subscribers or members, merely because there has been a restriction on entry, whether fees-based or not. Access to services such as the library, email or the managed learning environment (MLE) of many institutions is conditional upon having successfully enrolled, which requires the individual to have been accepted as a student and relevant fees to be paid. Although it is entirely possible to see this being implemented, most institutions do not yet distinguish between an enrolled student and one who has paid extra for 'premium' services.

Lam and Harrison-Walker, like Rappa, categorise e-business models, but do so using an objective-based typology. They differentiate the relevant dimensions between relational objectives and value-based objectives. Relational objectives are driven by the connectivity of the Internet – 'its ability to reach any user regardless of physical distance' (Lam and Harrison-Walker 2003: 20) – a unique property in comparison to physical delivery agents and physical product/service, to relate back to our adaptation of

Choi *et al.* above. Lam and Harrison-Walker further sub-divide relational objectives and value-based objectives as follows:

Relational objectives

- direct access – effectively disintermediation, that is, cutting out the middlemen between producer and consumer.
- network development – what we might term indirect relationships can be established among 'loosely connected groups and individuals' (2003: 21) that might not otherwise be connected. Lam and Harrison-Walker cite eBay as a primary example.
- corporate communication – providing information to existing or potential customers, to build demand for products/services or brand awareness.

Value-based objectives

- financial improvement – revenue streams are produced for a firm, either from user-paid (direct fees for users) or provider-paid (sponsored) activities.
- product and channel enrichment – aimed at producing loyalty and longer term relationships with users and thus producing value for the organisation, even if not delivering immediate financial gains.

Figure 4.5 shows the matrix of possible combinations of these two sets of objectives, by which means Lam and Harrison-Walker identify a range of e-business models. We will return to an application of the Lam and Harrison-Walker typology in Chapter 8.

Modelling post-compulsory education as an e-business

Fingar *et al.*'s (1999) framework (based on Porter's value chain as discussed above) has been adapted here (Figure 4.6) to provide an overview of four main areas that e-business can have some substantial impact upon within education. In the context of our adaptation of Choi *et al.*'s approach above, Figure 4.6 can be considered to be an alternative perspective on the virtual process 'plane' of Figure 4.3. The four quadrants in Figure 4.6, reflecting the different aspects of the provision of education services, from both a process and a product/service perspective, comprise:

1   **Information and knowledge market**
    Education may be viewed as intrinsically to do with the communication of information and knowledge, and e-enabled education offers new mechanisms by which to do this effectively and efficiently.

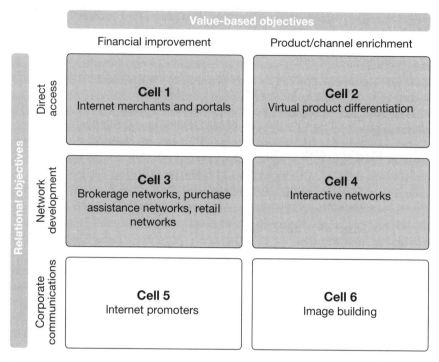

Figure 4.5 Objective-based typology of e-business models.

Source: adapted from Lam and Harrison-Walker 2003: 20.

2   Customer relationship management

One of the core themes from Chapter 3 – customer focus – is addressed in many e-businesses by a reorientation of business processes to reflect the customer perspective, in order to develop and sustain long-term, high-value relationships with customers. The provision of education services entails, by its very nature, a long-term relationship between provider and student.

3   Stakeholder relationship management

Educational institutions have a wide range of external stakeholders and have had to face increasing reporting pressures and accountability. This might be to research partners or funders, to QA and other compliance agencies, or to in-house and outsourced employees. Again, Web-mediated relationships with stakeholders provides opportunities for institutions to better cope with environmental pressures.

4   Supply Chain Management

We have already identified this core administrative area as one where educational institutions are already pursuing e-business practices, but

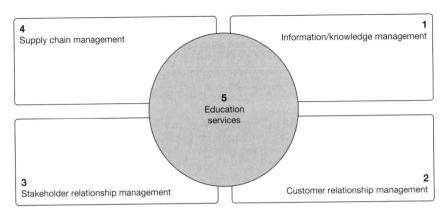

Figure 4.6 Web-enabled business processes for post-compulsory education.
Source: adapted from Fingar *et al.* 1999.

it remains a process that offers more opportunity for integration and development.

Each of these quadrants, then, reflects the underlying processes for delivering educational provision as well as the related services of granting of awards for educational achievement and the development of academic subject knowledge.

In each of these quadrants we can explore Lam and Harrison-Walker's relational and value objectives, relevant to the educational experience good and 'community model' variations of e-business – direct access, corporate communication, network development, financial improvement and product/channel enrichment – to see how these might indicate areas for improvement.

Each of these models, then, articulates e-business in a slightly different way, as they try to relate customers, stakeholders, networks and services. Each set of categorisations give a foundation for examining business processes within post-compulsory education, and allow some perspective on assessing the impact of e-business upon education. It is still 'early days' in deciding the efficacy of any of these approaches to an e-enabled post-compulsory education environment. However, some of the issues raised will be explored, using these models in greater detail, in Chapter 8 'Getting from here to there: improving processes and adding value'.

Conclusion

The intent behind this chapter has been to examine some of the analytical frameworks that have been applied to e-business and begin to map them to post-compulsory education. In so doing, we have explored a range of concerns, starting with the knotty issue of defining the nature of market relationships within education and moving to develop a framework for describing educational services in 'e-business space'. We have engaged with the foundations of the MIT 90s framework (Porter's value chain concept) and explored e-business models and their typology in relation to post-compulsory education.

The lessons to be absorbed from e-business practices are many, and an e-business approach has the potential to alter the traditional boundaries between individual educational institutions, and between private and public provision. It could reshape the way students, staff and other stakeholders and suppliers interact with each other. At the same time, there are other pressures already present in the education 'marketplace' which are likely to continue to develop and shape post-compulsory education in the future; most especially the globalisation of that marketplace and the growing impact of privatised educational services. The ways universities and colleges are already responding to this changing context is examined in the next chapter, together with a consideration of whether and how e-business approaches can help.

Note

1   See www2.nea.org/he/future/market.html.

Bibliography

Burnett, D. and Oblinger, D. (2002) *Innovation in Student Services: planning models for blending high touch/high tech*, Ann Arbor, MI: Society for College and University Planning (SCUP)/IBM.

Choi, S-Y, Stahl, D.O. and Whinston, A.B. (1997) *The Economics of Electronic Commerce*, Indianapolis, IN: Macmillan Technical Publishing.

Coombs, R. and Hull, R. (1997) 'The wider research context of Business Process Analysis' (Consultancy report for ESRC), Business Process Resources Centre, University of Warwick. Online. Available at http://scholar.google.com/scholar?hl=en&lr=&q=cache:A_6lS8rX4ewJ:bprc.warwick.ac.uk/umist1.html (accessed 15 December 2005).

Fingar, P. Kumar, H .and Sharma, T. (1999) '21st century markets: from places to spaces', *First Monday*, December 4 (12). Online. Available at www.firstmonday.dk/issues/issue4_12/fingar/index.html (accessed 15 December 2005).

Jelassi, T. and Enders, A. (2005) *Strategies for e-Business*, Harlow: FT Prentice-Hall.

Lam, Long W. and Harrison-Walker, L. Jean (2003) 'Towards an objective-based typology of e-business models', Business Horizons, November–December: 17–26.

Levine, A. (2000) 'Privatization in higher education', National Governors Association Online. Available at www.nga.org/cda/files/HIGHEREDPRIVATIZATION.pdf (accessed 8 December 2005).

Lipsey, R. and Chrystal, A. (2004) *Economics*, 10th edn, Oxford, Oxford University Press.

Matkin, G. (2002) 'Developing a conceptual framework and vocabulary for e-learning' in *Teaching as E-business? Research and Policy Agendas.* Selected Conference Proceedings, Centre for Studies in Higher Education (CSHE) (2002), University of California, Berkeley. Paper CSHE3–0. Online. Available at http:// repositories.cdlib.org/cshe/CSHE3–01 (accessed 5 December 2006).

Mintzberg, H. Ahlstrand, B. and Lampel, J. (1998) *Strategy Safari*, London: FT-Prentice Hall.

National Education Association, 'Market driven futures', NEA.org Online. Available at www2.nea.org/he/future/market.html (accessed 15 December 2005).

Nelson, Philip (1970) 'Information and consumer behaviour', *Journal of Political Economy* 78 (2): 311–29.

NOIE (2002) 'e-Business in education', *DCITA*, June. Online. Available at www.dcita.gov.au/ie/publications/2002/june/ebusiness_in_education (accessed 15 December 2005).

Osterwalder, A. and Pigneur, Y. (2002) 'An e-Business model ontology for modeling e-business', 15th Bled Electronic Commerce Conference – e-Reality: Constructing the e-Economy (Bled, Slovenia), 17–19 June.

Pateli, A. and Giaglis, M. (2004) 'A research framework for analyzing e-Business models', *European Journal of Information Systems* 13: 302–14.

Porter, M. (1985) *Competitive Advantage: creating and sustaining superior performance*, New York: The Free Press.

Porter, M. (2001) 'Strategy and the Internet', *Harvard Business Review*, March. Also available online at www.sfu.ca/~anthonyc/cmpt301/301_case_files/pr/porter. pdf (accessed 05 December 2006).

Rappa, M. (2005) 'Business models on the web', *digitalenterprise.org*, 1 May. Online. Available at http://digitalenterprise.org/models/models.html (accessed 3 May 2005).

Chapter 5

Educational services and the global marketplace

Jos Boys and Karen Stanton

Education and training (whether virtual, conventional or hybrid) is a market increasingly targeted by for-profit organisations, both to supply their own internal training needs and for revenue generation. These may be corporate or public (such as the NHS), online learning providers (such as Phoenix) or campus-based suppliers. How is post-compulsory education in the UK responding to these challenges? What will be the long-term educational impact – both on the student experience and on the 'shape' of institutions? And can applying the e-business approach of customer focus, organisational integration and common systems offer some clues as to productive ways forward?

The growth of consortia

Universities and colleges have responded to the increasing globalisation and privatisation of post-compulsory education by developing consortia – both to take advantage of the opportunities offered and to compete more effectively in this changing context. Consortia have enabled the development of new campuses and/or courses organised across national boundaries. In addition, the steadily increasing demand for e-learning in the USA and worldwide has encouraged the development of high-level consortia to allow the sharing of course materials that are expensive for an individual institution to produce.[1]

The most famous of these, led by MIT Open Courseware, is a complex stitching together of many different universities. It comprises Johns Hopkins, University of Michigan, Tufts, Utah State, Harvard Law School, Rice and Foothill-de Anza Community College from the USA; with the Universities of Tokyo, Kyoto, Keio and Waseda and the Tokyo Institute of Technology from Japan; the Universities of Barcelona and de las Islas Baleares from Spain; and Peking University, Tsinghua University, Beijing Jiaotong University, Dalian University of Technology, Central South University, Shanghai Jiaotong University, Xi'an Jiaotong University, Central Radio and

TV University, Sichuan University, Nanjing University and Harbin Institute of Industry and Technology from China.

Distance learning is already thriving in the US. The Sloan Consortium's 2005 research report *Growing by Degrees: Online Education in the US* showed a growth from 1.98 million in 2003 to 2.35 million the following year, more than ten times that predicted by the National Centre for Educational Statistics for the general post-compulsory student population. The success and enthusiasm for e-learning in the US, combined with the desire to widen worldwide access to higher education, also underpinned the creation of U21 Global. Established in 1999 and backed by 16 members of the successful international consortium Universitas 21 and Thomson Learning, it launched its first online MBA programme in Spring 2003.

The Observatory on Borderless Higher Education (2005) reported that to date some 400 students from 25 countries were enrolled with a further 1,400 applications waiting to be processed. It could be argued that although enrolments are at a relatively low level to date, increased applications are an indicator of success and that by focusing on clearly specified online products for mainly the Asian and Middle Eastern regions, U21 Global has sensibly drawn from the US experience to concentrate its efforts on an appropriate target market. As of 2006, after two and a half years of operation, U21 Global's MBA programme, for example, had 1,300 students. The Observatory report predicts that enrolments and course offerings are likely to increase at a modest pace over time along with increased brand recognition and reputation.

This growth is enabled both because of the ubiquity of the Web and because its nature is changing – from informational, structured and one-way teaching materials to networked and interactive communication. As Richard Straub, president of the European e-Learning Industry Group says, 'e-learning has moved from formal information to a much more informal, integrated type of learning' (*Financial Times* 20 March 2006).

Mature target markets may, however, be crucial for success. Simon Marginson of Monash University (Marginson 2004) has strongly argued that virtual universities have not attracted higher levels of enrolments faster because an online degree is a less attractive qualification than a face-to-face degree acquired in a foreign country or the campus of a foreign university in the student's country. Evidence to date from the Higher Education Funding Council (HEFCE) e-China programme, attests to the desire in China, at least, for a more blended approach to e-learning with face-to-face tutorials. In China, as in many other countries, there is also a need to build public confidence in e-learning. Another cautionary tale is the experience of the UK Open University (OU) when it tried to extend its distance learning courses into the US. Despite being a recognised high-quality brand across Europe and elsewhere, they were unsuccessful in taking the OU model to America, probably because of underestimating the amount of start-up funding required, the difficulties of regulation in a federalised country and the unwillingness of American students to take on academic products built on a British approach to history and culture.

In addition, although the growth in distance learning in the US has almost all been within its own domestic market, educational providers from outside the US mainly aim to operate globally, raising many issues of language, culture and time differences.

Overall, then, for-profit organisations are beginning to make inroads in to the traditional domain of universities and colleges. What do we need to know about these competitors in the changing UK context and how should post-compulsory institutions respond effectively?

The competitors

David Collis, Fredrick Frank adjunct Professor of International Business Administration at Yale University, proposes five key elements that seem to have the greatest repercussions for traditional colleges and universities: the courses new players offer; their target customer group; where their content originates; the pedagogy they employ; and their pricing (Collis 2000).

In 2000, he argued that new entrants into the American market are predominantly providing business-related materials. Of the companies he studied, 75 per cent were providing courses in management, performance improvement and skills related to employment, such as information technology. Of the remainder, a large proportion were offering courses to lawyers and doctors, focusing on continuing professional development. In addition, most of these were at postgraduate rather than undergraduate level. In a way this is obvious: these are the most immediately lucrative and receptive markets for an entry strategy. Collis suggests that:

> as firms build brand names and establish presence in the market, one can predict an evolution in course offerings from short management certificates and continuing education for the professions through more general and softer leadership skills and performance improvement, to an MBA or other professional degree, and only finally into undergraduate liberal arts degrees.
>
> (2000: 12)

Currently, the primary audience for these players is business, one of the largest and fastest growing areas of the post-compulsory education market. It is also often well-suited to online learning, although, as with the experience of conventional universities, completion rates are improved where tutors are also involved face-to-face, or through an equivalent 'virtual' method such as conferencing.

Collis then explored the three alternative sources of educational content for commercial entrants into the education market: hiring their own staff; licensing existing courses from colleges and universities; and contracting directly with individual academics (similar to the existing system for publishing academic books). As he says:

> The data suggests that entrants are keeping their sourcing options open. Indeed, several major players seem to be pursuing all three options. While deals at the university level are attractive, thus far they have been quite expensive: the long-term trend will probably be for entrants to source materials directly from faculty.
>
> (2000: 13)

This also means that, as with conventional provision, there is no 'standard' pedagogic approach across new commercial providers.

Finally, Collis argues that pricing strategies have the greatest potential to disturb higher education's current environment. This is particularly true of the potential of online learning – new technologies should allow for very low-priced courses, since the marginal cost of delivering it (after the initial investment) could be negligible. However, he also suggests that new entrants to the market will not want to undermine its existing cost structure for customers, and that education remains an experience good (as outlined in Chapter 4), that is, one that is also about the perception and supply of quality and not just price. Others, however, are not so convinced by the 'first mover' argument that these new players will have the advantage in expanding into other areas beyond the lucrative ones of business studies and computing.[2]

Moving to two extremes?

Many authors argue that the changing context of education is forcing it into two alternative directions: a 'low end', which emphasises standardised services and ease of access, versus a 'high end', which builds on brand status and quality of materials. A *Financial Times* report on Distance Learning MBAs argued that the main difference is between universities who want to build on their existing courses and brands and those that start from the needs of the workplace manager, that is, who design new courses which are explicitly workplace-based: 'For the first group, rigour and accreditation are the main selling points. For the second, scale and flexibility are paramount' (*Financial Times* 20 March 2006).

Terry Hilsberg of NextEd Ltd, using the work of Christensen and Raynor (2003) argues that existing post-compulsory educational providers tend to work from an 'internal' perspective; that is they work from their own internal drivers and not from the demands of customers (Hilsberg 2004). Any changes in educational approach or structure are therefore concentrated in an additive process of sustaining innovations, rather than by challenging or disrupting existing frameworks (see Figure 5.1).

According to Christensen and Raynor, the alternative response of low-end disruption usually occurs where existing customers' needs can be meet with a lower cost business model, that is, by offering lower prices and better margins for equivalent quality. This can mean, for example, standardisation of the components of a product and its processes, which in turn may allow a disaggregation of the whole value chain (see Chapter 4). Hilsberg argues that some community colleges, Asian private colleges and Open Universities internationally have low-cost production processes compared to services provided by the western HE sector, laden with overheads (50 per cent in many cases) and with research expenses. They can make money by slightly undercutting fees compared to these courses and by being able to disaggregate the conventional HE supply chain. This is by both standardising components across courses (similar curricula and textbooks for example) and by working to common standards and systems, such as well-developed credit precedent databases, articulation agreements and standard qualifications frameworks. Meanwhile the speed and connectivity of Web-enabled services allows customised access to potential customers globally.

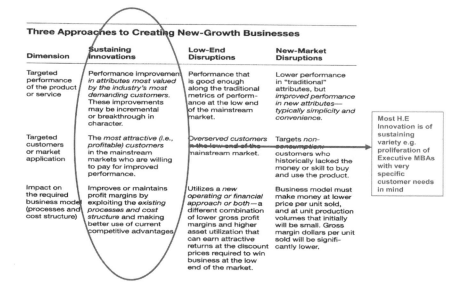

Figure 5.1 Approaches to growth: the conventional HE approach.

Source: Hilsberg 2004, adapted from Christensen and Raynor 2003.

Hilsberg argues that the 'economic sweet spot' here initially lies with low-cost providers (such as Malaysian colleges). However, as educational services become more commoditised and competitive, the commercial edge will move to those with 'a scarce good', namely those with accreditation and award-giving powers who can offer 'brand quality' to the post-compulsory market. Hilsberg suggests that this is exactly what is happening in Asian and Australian college and university education, the areas in which his company, NextEd Ltd, operates. But he also says that these struggles over the market continue to shift and notes that the Chinese universities (who control through central planning where their students go) now 'increasingly want to own the whole Western value chain'. We will return to this issue later in this chapter, in relation to University of Nottingham's involvement with the HEFCE e-China initiative.

At the 'high end', the MIT Open Knowledge Initiative (OKI) and its consortia have already been mentioned. Here, universities can sell their 'brand' quality, and most especially the worldwide renown and expertise of particular academics. In this model, the aim is often to produce very high-quality online materials (for example, streaming media of lectures by world-renowned experts in specific subjects, supported by high-quality animations, etc.), which can be viewed globally and supported by teaching assistants in different locations.

HE and FE institutions in the UK will have their own take on these 'extremes' and how they want to place themselves in relation to other commercial and public organisations, both as competitors and collaborators. These opportunities also need to be reviewed in relation to the changing UK educational context.

A changing approach to educational services in the UK?

HEFCE has recently re-released its e-learning strategy following the demise of its e-university project, UKeU (Slater 2005). The failure of UKeU has been attributed to poor market research and a failure to identify student needs; poor leadership; too much concentration and investment in the technology, i.e. a customised learning platform; a large number of overseas offices; too large a number of high brand programmes; and a substantial and costly central London presence (Brennan and Papatsiba 2004).

Based on the work of Slater (2005), the following lessons can be learnt from the problems of UKeU and from the failure of the OU in the US (already mentioned above):

- keep to simple models in line with normal procedures;
- have a clear view of the market;
- spend a modest amount on the development of a platform;

- build in early formative evaluation;
- concentrate where gains are greatest;
- share activities and development wherever it is feasible and realistic;
- have enthusiastic and motivated internal management of process.

Many of these elements have long been identified as success factors underpinning e-learning in the US, much of which has been delivered entirely online to large numbers of students, with evidence of success and underpinned by a conviction that e-learning is at least as pedagogically sound as conventional approaches (Observatory on Borderless Higher Education 2005). Highly successful online learning programmes, especially in terms of student enrolments, have been reported in public universities such as Johns Hopkins, Penn State and the University of Baltimore, and in private universities such as the University of Phoenix and Dallas Baptist University. The materials cover all possible combinations of topics. The top six success factors identified in the US were:

- motivation (focus on student needs);
- commitment of key people and resources (focus on strengths);
- measurement of progress;
- student and staff enthusiasm;
- provision of an enhanced educational product;
- a programmed approach (complete online courses rather than modules or blended learning).

(OBHE 2005)

It could be argued that the success of wholly online programmes in the US has only been possible there because there is a more mature market for online post-compulsory education. The Pew Survey of the Internet in the US recently found that students there firmly believe that the Internet has enhanced their education (Pew Survey 2006). In response to a slower take-up in the UK, the revised HEFCE strategy for e-development in higher education was wide-ranging and aspirational with a long payback period. (HEFCE 2005). It encouraged universities to continue to progress in the area of e-learning provision on their own, within a supported framework of national advice and guidance from the Joint Information Systems Committee (JISC) and the new Higher Education Academy (HEA). As of 2005, HEFCE had provided funding for 74 Centres of Excellence in Teaching and Learning (CETLs), many of which focus on practice development involving ICT. JISC provides support and funding for innovation and developments in technology and the cost-effective use of ICT; and the HEA provides guidance for developing the e-learning skills of academic staff.

HEFCE's new model for e-learning focuses on developing the e-learning skills of staff. It recommends that universities focus upon enhancing infrastructure to embed practice within institutions across all disciplines and activities, with delivery on or near a campus but at a learner chosen time and place and with appropriate pedagogy.

Following the report to HEFCE by the Centre for Higher Education Research and Information (Brennan and Papatsiba 2004) the strategy also stresses the need for further research into how students learn using new technologies. The UK's new policy and funding framework and the proposed model for e-learning therefore privileges blended approaches (part face-to-face; part interactive multimedia; part self-directed online, etc.). This recognises the student demand for high-quality learning products that make the best use of new technologies. It also identifies additional opportunities provided by e-learning environments for widening access, self-directed learning, lifelong learning, online assessment and student choice at any age. We will return to these two key issues of staff development (changing organisational roles) and student experience later in this chapter.

The Becta post-compulsory e-learning strategy

The FE and schools sectors illustrate the broader approach within which an e-learning strategy can be developed – offering up goals for all citizens, not just students at university or college. Its outcomes directly reflect the six priorities in the Department for Education and Skills (DfES) e-strategy 'Harnessing technology: transforming learning and children's services'[3] with one additional outcome specific to the post-compulsory sector: ICT user skills for life. It lists intended outcomes of its ICT strategy as follows:

Priority 1 An integrated online information service for all citizens.
Priority 2 Integrated online personal support for children and learners.
Priority 3 A collaborative approach to personalised learning activities.
Priority 4 A good-quality training and support package for practitioners.
Priority 5 A leadership and development package for organisational capability in ICT.
Priority 6 A common digital infrastructure to support transformation and reform ICT user skills for life.

In the FE context there has been a range of initiatives concerned, for example, with using ICT to support the development of regional centres. At the same time, as already outlined, FE is already in much more direct competition with private providers, particularly for work-based training. The biggest of these private companies, Carter and Carter, has, as of 2006, been buying up smaller competitors. Peter Marples, their group business development director, was reported in *The Guardian* newspaper as saying that his company will be working with colleges some of the time and in competition at other times – 'that is the nature of a mature market' (*The Guardian* 21 March 2006).

This is the local context, then, in which universities and colleges must plan for fully integrating ICT into everything they do. We have already touched on the potential impact of the globalisation of post-compulsory educational provision. We now need to explore this further. The internationalisation of the HE sector (and the regionalisation of the FE sector), combined with both the increasing diversification of students across different cultures and experiences, and their increasing ICT literacy and demand for quality online provision, signals the need for a new phase of strategic activity. Whether the scale of diversity is relatively local or more explicitly global, universities and colleges are now increasingly dealing with a wide range of students across multiple physical and virtual sites. Institutions will have to consider the implications for student experiences and stakeholder relationships. They will have to explore how to develop the new kinds of academic and administrative roles required of staff so that they can engage with curriculum development and delivery on a potentially global scale, with all that implies in terms of 24/7 tutorial and administrative support, hybrid means of delivery and different cultural norms, educational methods, quality control and regulation. Here, again, the key e-business issues are customer focus, organisational integration and common standards. To complete this chapter, we will look briefly at each of these issues in turn.

Changing students, changing services?

It has already been noted that the commercial organisations who have come to educational services 'afresh' (such as Phoenix or NextEd) are well aware of the importance of customer focus and have invested in new types of 24/7 telephone, email or conferencing-based student support systems as a central component of their services. This has implications both for traditional patterns of teaching and learning, and for conventional academic/student services/administrative roles. In addition, it suggests that we can still find out more about how different students learn effectively, and what sorts of educational support they need at various stages of that learning. The Learning Sciences Research Institute (LSRI) at the University of Nottingham, for example, is developing a research project examining both the operational and cultural issues of supporting students on their Chinese campus at Ningbo (see Box 5.1). Some US universities are explicitly connecting the design of these different forms of educational delivery and development to a widening participation agenda.

At the same time, many institutions are exploring the buying, selling, sharing and reusing of educational content to support students at different locations, across older institutional boundaries and to develop economies of scale. Although many government and other funded projects are still

Box 5.1   Learning how people e-learn in China

Project

China has a population of 1.6 billion people. The government sees e-learning technology as a means of providing cost-effective education. Its 68 e-learning institutions, however, have experienced varying levels of success. As part of the Chinese government's initiative to meet this vast social need, the LSRI has been collaborating with Beijing Foreign Studies University over the last three years to discover the most effective methods of learning within 21st-century Chinese culture.*

The work is funded by the HEFCE 'e-China UK' programme. Its remit is to encourage collaboration and mutual understanding between academics in both countries. The programme includes a number of projects focused on the joint development of learning materials and involves other UK universities such as Cambridge, Manchester and Southampton.

Process transformation and project implementation

The University of Nottingham has an established Malaysian campus in Kuala Lumpur and more recently has been operating a physical campus in the City of Ningbo near Shanghai (an area designated for future development). In 2005 it received a licence from the Chinese Ministry of Education to offer undergraduate and masters programmes. It already has 1,000 Chinese students who want an authentic University of Nottingham experience but delivered more cost effectively at the local level – the core aim of the university. The LSRI is helping the university to deliver its courses and safeguard it standards.

Academic activities at Ningbo are processed through relevant teaching committees to maintain the intellectual rigour and depth of the Nottingham brand, but some processes have needed to be changed to comply with local regulations. The LSRI is now being encouraged to build a research centre on the Ningbo campus to extend its joint investigations into the social, scientific and psychological bases of human learning.

As the University of Nottingham looks at infrastructure issues for supporting networked learning across all campuses (such as accessing the library electronically), it is using the LSRI to address questions such as how resources can be linked internationally yet retain a sense of belonging at the local level, and how best to supervise PhD students from the UK. The LSRI is exploring solutions for using technology powerfully but non-obtrusively to enhance processes of teaching, learning and research.

Main challenges

Although academic culture tends to be similar throughout the world, there are cultural and regulatory differences that need to be appreciated across different nationalities.

The LSRI needs to explore the barriers that hinder a joint understanding of how people think and learn and how this differs in the UK and China. The nature of the subject is proving of specific interest to post cultural-revolutionary Chinese society and this is helping the process.

Benefits

- Learning Science is a unique inter-disciplinary subject that brings together Psychology, Computer Science and Education and the LSRI is recognised as an international leader in the type of fundamental research that can address the issues faced by both the University of Nottingham as it expands its international campuses and the Chinese in finding the most efficient methods for raising educational standards across its vast population.
- The group of collaborating institutions is now seeking to design the most effective models for blended learning.
- The LSRI will be promoting an international student exchange programme between the UK and Ningbo.
- The University of Nottingham and the LSRI are gaining strong intellectual benefits by working with the Chinese.

*More information is available from: www.nottingham.ac.uk/lsri and
www.nottingham.edu.cn/classaction/progtech/newsdee.asp

struggling to persuade the HE and FE communities to share educational materials, some progress has been made. For example, the Universities Consortium of e-Learning (UCeL) was founded in March 2002 as a multi-institutional collective to collaboratively produce and share high-quality interactive multimedia resources for health-professional education. Its six founding partners, the Universities of Cambridge, Nottingham, Manchester, East Anglia, Wolverhampton and Peninsula Medical School (Plymouth/Exeter) offer a wide range of subjects supported by UCeL resources: medicine, nursing, pharmacy, behavioural sciences, sports science and health studies.[4]

Similarly, the Learning Resource Catalogue (LRC) is an EDTeC initiative that has been endorsed by the U21 Consortium. The LRC provides the mechanism for academics at the University of New South Wales (UNSW) and other U21 collegial institutions to manage and share their teaching resources online. As such, the LRC represents a means of collegial interaction for the purpose of providing learning resources (learning objects) for students at all levels. When managing their learning resources with the LRC, academics may simply share the resources within UNSW or, if they wish, they may submit for sharing across the U21 network. Such materials are visible to all LRC users at all institutions.[5]

Others are examining the extent to which learning can be broken down into smaller reusable learning objects (RLOs) or chunks, which can be adapted within different modules and modes of delivery.[6] Rather than constructing a whole module or course, very high-quality interactive media elements can be designed to be adapted by different teachers in different contexts. One example from one of the collaborators, the School of Nursing at the University of Nottingham, used RLOs to reduce costs in teaching elements of nursing (see Box 5.2).

The importance of staff development

Some of the issues for changing staff roles have already been covered. In addition, as Open University Business School director of programmes and curriculum, Professor Mark Fenton O'Creevy has noted:

> People massively underestimate the upfront effort and production of good quality learning materials [in creating a successful programme].
> (*Financial Times* 20 March 2006)

There are also considerable implications for staff skills and development. This may be in dealing with diverse groups of students from different backgrounds through a variety of media, or exploring the teaching and learning methods appropriate to distance learning. For example, Professor Gilly Salmon (an expert on e-moderation) has produced a staff development programme at Leicester University aimed at helping academics understand e-conferencing (see Box 5.3). Another example was developed by research staff at City University, London, who wanted to improve the productivity of part-time teaching staff delivering a large, open access evening programme of short courses for adult learners. The existing staff development programme was aimed at full-time staff based on attendance at workshops; instead a virtual learning environment (VLE) was developed 'not based on the results of deficit audit but . . . from a developmental culture', which:

> must take account of the social and political contexts within which teaching takes place at a time of dwindling resources and burgeoning managerial culture; and (which) should reinforce teacher autonomy and expertise.
> (Patel and Mangan 2005: 140)

Box 5.2 Collaboration reduces the cost of multi-media learning

Project: Reusable Learning Objects (RLOs)

The project's principal aim was to see how educational institutions could work together to produce high-cost multimedia e-learning materials economically. The partners included:

- School of Nursing, Queens Medical Centre
- Centre for Applied Research in Educational Technology (CARET), University of Cambridge
- Learning Technology Research Institute, London Metropolitan University

Process transformation and project implementation

The educational value of good quality multimedia is well recognised, but typical production costs put them beyond the reach of single institutions. The future, as the School of Nursing discovered, is through collaboration. This began as an informal working relationship between three institutions, which was subsequently formalised as a Centre of Excellence in April 2005 when Queens School of Nursing won HEFCE project funding. This newly formalised partnership is an example of a 'bottom-up'* process of change.

The endeavour had modest beginnings in the mid 1990s when the School started producing Computer Assisted Learning (CAL) packages. The team quickly recognised, however, that these were too long and not easy to use. Heather Wharrad, the project leader, decided that a standard format had to be established with the criterion that any Learning Object had to address a single learning objective. The format allowed for content, interactive elements and self assessment.

This approach became one of the critical success factors because it put a natural time limit on each RLO, improving the quality of learning. Academic staff also found the process easy to engage with compared with earlier e-learning materials. Process evolution led to a series of RLO design templates. This is an ongoing process that seeks to establish the most effective cross-institution pedagogical solutions.

Main challenges

The University of Nottingham's School of Nursing attracts professional hospital staff from nursing practice who enrol for post-registration courses.

Typically, these are short eight-week Continuous Professional Development (CPD) courses. The students need to understand the physiology of new generation pharmaceuticals but may not have formally studied chemistry and biology for many years. The challenge is to prepare these students quickly so that they can assimilate knowledge effectively within a much shorter period of time than full-time undergraduates. At the undergraduate level, the School is preparing RLOs for teaching statistics, which some nursing students find difficult but which will be adaptable to meet the requirements of different subject disciplines in the other partner institutions.

Having shown that its RLOs work well at the micro level (ie in a single subject discipline within a single institution) the School now has to prove that the materials can be reused by the other partners for their own teaching contexts as well as having broader value when made accessible through a digital repository (macro level). Collaboration is essential if a learning object is to have genuine cross-institutional value.

Another challenge of collaboration is to define ways of working so that the most suitable partner is identified for developing a particular Learning Object. Each partner then works from a position of strength.

Benefits

The Pharmacology RLOs are now being used nationally and internationally as the school is receiving positive feedback from across the UK, Paris and Dublin. The CPD courses currently run six times a year in five different centres.

The next step is to extend RLO best practice and share the benefits of collaboration by attracting more partners from both the FE and HE sectors. Eduserv Foundation funding will help accelerate this process. Future RLOs will focus on issues such as Infections Control and Prescribing.

The School has now employed a full time Learning Technologist. The expertise of the technologist has helped the School avoid making mistakes and so contributed to the bottom line as well as enhanced team working with academics.

*See www.rlo-cetl.ac.uk

Box 5.3 Uniting online immigrants and digital natives

Project: Developing a staff development programme, University of Leicester

Many hold the view that technology is the key to creating a successful online learning environment. When the University of Leicester recognised that communication and collaboration were such important factors, it introduced a structured staff development programme to achieve a successful online capability.

Process transformation and project implementation

According to Professor Salmon,* working online with groups creates both a psychological and sociological environment that is different to that experienced in face-to-face teaching. It is a more democratic environment where time operates differently. Academic staff that are new to online teaching need to know how best to exploit the medium and this demands new skills.

In the early days, training focused on menu items within a VLE rather than on how to teach, support or interact with students. Staff used notice boards to encourage discussion but without any mechanisms to make this happen. In face-to-face teaching these highly capable people would structure activities and pace them, give feedback to students and enable groups to work together.

Since online teaching requires new skills, the University organised a staff development programme that includes both formal and informal training. For example, the university's 'Certificate in Academic Practice' course, which all new teaching staff have to complete, now includes a major section about teaching online. Less formal courses are also run to help staff born before the digital generation (immigrants) and those born into it (natives) to acquire these skills and prevent a divide developing between them.

The training shows staff how to choose media for different educational purposes and how to exploit the massive amount of online resources, and provides a framework for managing people's behaviour, but most importantly how to operate in online groups.

Main challenges

The key challenge was to bring about a cultural change. New skills cannot be achieved in a half-day training course. This involved engaging in discussion about what people understand about learning and teaching. The University had to deal with subject groups such as fine art, sciences and others who had very specific views about how teaching should be delivered.

Benefits

- Students at Leicester who attend formal lectures benefit from much greater flexibility with 24/7 broadband access to learning resources.
- The University found that an old method of learning, the case study, developed by Harvard University for its MBA course, works far more effectively in an online environment where students engage more deeply with resources and gain a much better understanding from the case study.
- When a lecturer in engineering became Pro Vice Chancellor but wanted to continue teaching to second and third year undergraduates, he started putting his material into a VLE and used a bulletin board for student communication. This has produced better examination results year on year since 2003. Now the Pro Vice Chancellor is adding mobile learning to the mix by developing an MP3 file for the VLE, which is updated every week. Students download the file to their iPods and listen to his new assignment instructions when, for example, travelling on the bus to the campus.
- Leicester Online has 7,000 students, who are primarily based overseas. All their learning resources are delivered through a VLE, which is transforming the students' ability to study – and it is not a second-class experience.

* More information about Gilly Salmon's work can be seen by visiting: www.e-tivities.com, www.le.ac.uk/beyonddistance, www.atimod.com, www.atimod.com/presentations, and www.e-moderating.com

Patel and Mangan were particularly aware of the difficulties of enabling buy-in among part-time staff for staff development and of defining productivity (both in terms of quality and student retention, progression and achievement). The resulting online staff development product (Ambient) was thus able to allow staff to relate to their own particular interests, performance and needs, and to learn 'just-in time' rather than as part of the academic calendar.

Using new technologies effectively

The e-business model emphasises the importance of common technological standards for common processes. The University of Nottingham, for example, developed two portals, one aimed at prospective undergraduates (winner of the UCISA Award 2005) and one at prospective postgraduates, to enable it to communicate effectively with applicants and students. These portals are integrated with the Nottingham-based website to explicitly link and offer equivalent sets of student experience. Links to the Malaysian and China campuses are also available from this top-level of the website.

At the more local level, Tamworth and Lichfield College was asked to become the Virtual Learning Centre for the Staffordshire region, to share e-learning infrastructure and content. In this case the main challenge was to integrate effectively with learndirect (see Box 5.4). Here, the College had to develop interoperability between non-common systems.

Education, business and the marketplace

In a 2006 *Financial Times* report, the newspaper compared distance learning providers for the MBA; worldwide the University of Phoenix came top with 40,000 students a year, the Edinburgh Business School at Herriot-Watt University second with 8,922. Both of these have rolling programmes, with new recruits taken on each week. At number 24 was the Euro MBA consortium with 35 students a year, based on six residential weeks across Europe. This, then, represents a range of activities and approaches (*Financial Times* 3 March 2006).

Hilsberg argues that as the HE sector becomes increasingly 'marketised' (whether it wants to or not), the issues of global competition and changing institutional roles will become much more central to UK university and college decision-making. David Collis, whose overview of new commercial entrants into education was summarised at the beginning of this chapter, proposes that the demands of the corporate market have enabled new commercial providers to develop faster, more responsively and to build better capability than conventional providers. And he says:

> Two important conclusions can be drawn. [. . .] The first is that the direct competitive threat to most of the traditional offerings of colleges and universities will be delayed. Instead entrants are largely focused on the corporate market and graduate training level, and at only slightly lower prices. This is the good news.
>
> The bad news is that well funded competitors, often backed by brand named institutions through alliances, will be hard to beat once they are established. First mover advantage that they can exploit, particularly the more rapid development of skills needed to harness the new technologies and develop new pedagogies, will put them in good stead as they gradually transition to compete more directly in the traditional higher education market.
>
> (Hilsberg 2004)

This chapter has highlighted some of the considerable amount of both strategic development and individual project initiatives that are already taking place across the UK. It has shown aspects of the increasing expertise

Box 5.4 Simple college portal adds value to e-learning materials

Project: Implementing a Virtual Learning Centre (VLC)

Tamworth & Lichfield College wanted to establish a community of e-learning and offer an alternative experience to conventional learning.

Process transformation and project implementation

Virtual learning was originally promoted as a concept amongst all the FE institutions within the Staffordshire University Regional Federation (SURF). As a result, the Lichfield campus was set up as a joint venture between the University of Staffordshire and Lichfield College as a centre for e-learning, using learndirect (LD) materials. A niche market was identified and targeted with EDCL and National Tests in Literacy online courses.

One year later, the college was asked to become the VLC for the whole of Staffordshire region because it had developed its own highly robust support systems. It has since gained an additional contract from the University for Industry (UFI) to extend its coverage to Shropshire and the Welsh Borders and down to Surrey.

Main challenges

The LD MLE crashed frequently as it struggled to support students and so Lichfield College set up its own website and loaded LD materials into it. This was the principal success factor. Security within Microsoft Internet Explorer, however, created technical problems. It prevented home learners from accessing course exercises and it blocked pop-ups that LD uses extensively in its materials. Lichfield College website created a more robust learner support system, overcame the pop-up issue and used email for communication between learners and tutors.

From the website, students can enrol online, receive advice and access both LD courses and additional learner resources. The college solved all the technical challenges so effectively, that all student surveys show a 90%-plus satisfaction rating. Main challenges for the future will be caused by changes in funding regulations, which will price courses beyond the means of many people who typically enrol on these courses.

Benefits

* The college has experienced exponential growth in online student enrolments.

- The EDCL course runs 12-15 months with a 100% successful completion in 2005.
- The college has amassed extensive experience in relating ICT needs to education.
- High-quality learning materials are better than the college is able to resource cost effectively in-house.
- Excellent relationships between learners and tutors.
- Development of high-quality communication skills.

in providing post-compulsory education both regionally and across a global marketplace. Next, we will attempt to put this in the wider context of UK HE and FE educational provision. How effective are these institutions in using emerging technologies in support of their overall aims and objectives? As the next chapter asks, 'Where are we now?'

Notes

1   See Johnstone, S. (2005) 'Trends in North American e-learning'. LearnTec. Online. Available at www.wcet.info/resources/staffpresentations.
2   See Simon Marginson of Monash University in Rood, D. (2004) 'Online universities failed to make the grade', *Sydney Morning Herald*, 15 November. See also, Michael Goldstein 'The economics of e-learning', in *Teaching as E-business? Research and Policy Agendas*. Selected Conference Proceedings Centre for Studies in Higher Education (CSHE), University of California, Berkeley, 2002, pp.13–20 for an alternative view.
3   See Becta. Online. Available at www.becta.org.uk/post16elearningstrategy/index.cfm.
4   See Universities Consortium of e-Learning (UCeL). Online. Available at www.ucel.ac.uk/about/Default.html.
5   See LRC. Online. Available at www.edtec.unsw.edu.au/frames_inter.cfm?area=2&page=S_LRC.cfm.
6   See *Centre for Excellence in Teaching and Learning (CETL) in Reuseable Learning Objects (RLOs)*, London Metropolitan University. Online. Available at www.rlo-cetl.ac.uk.

Bibliography

Brennan, J., Knight, P. and Papatsiba, V. (2004) 'Towards a research strategy on teaching and learning'. Report to HEFCE by CHEI, London.
Christensen, Clayton M. and Raynor, Michael E. (2003) *The Innovator's Solution: creating and sustaining successful growth*. Boston, MA: Harvard Business School Press.

Collis, D. (2000) 'New business models for higher education'. Online. Available at www.educause.edu/ir/library/pdf/ffp0101s.pdf (accessed 05 December 2006).

Financial Times (2006) 'Special report: business education', 20 March.

Hilsberg, T. (2004) 'Will universities become extinct in the networked world?' NextEd Ltd, 21st ICDE World Conference Paper, February. Online. Available at www.nexted.com/nexted/white-papers/8/default.pdf (accessed 5 December 2006).

HEFCE (2005) 'Strategy for e-development in higher education'. Online. Available at www.hefce.ac.uk/pubs/HEFCE/2005/05_12/ (accessed 5 December 2006).

Marginson, S. (2004) 'Don't leave me hanging on the anglophone: the potential for online distance higher education in the Asia-Pacific region.' *Higher Education Quarterly* 58 (2–3): 74–113. Blackwell Synergy.

Observatory on Borderless Higher Education (2004) 'Breaking news: update on universitas 21 global – another e-university destined to failure?' 7 December.

Observatory on Borderless Higher Education (2005) 'Breaking news: US study of e-learning at 21 universities and colleges seeks to isolate success factors' 13 February.

Patel, U. and Mangan, P. (2005) 'Using soft-system management methodology to develop an online part-time staff development resource', in Groccia, J.E. and Miller, J.E. (eds) *On Becoming a Productive University: strategies for reducing costs and increasing quality in higher education.* Bolton, MA: Anker Publishing Company Inc.

Pew Internet and American Life Project Survey (2006) 30 November 2005 to 4 April. Results are based on a non-random Web-based survey. Online. Available at http://news.bbc.co.uk/1/shared/bsp/hi/pdfs/22_09_2006pewsummary.pdf (accessed 5 December 2006).

Slater, J. (2005) 'Spent force on revolution in progress? E-learning after the e-university'. London: Higher Education Policy Institute Working Paper.

Spencer-Oatey, H. (2005) 'Sino-British collaboration to develop e-learning course-ware. A work-in-progress report on overarching issues'. Report of the E-China Sino-UK e-learning programme.

Chapter 6

Where are we now?

Les Watson

Like other organisations, post-compulsory educational institutions are under constant pressure from technological, economic, social and organisational change. Such change is inevitable. The challenge is how to take control, respond to and anticipate change, so as to fit the organisation better for the environment in which it exists. If the pace of change really is greater than ever before then organisations must adapt and evolve more rapidly than ever before, not only to keep up but also to take advantage of their changing internal and external environments and to improve their competitive position. The promise of ICT is that it can enable an organisation to adapt rapidly to the changing environment. This concept of the adaptive enterprise, which draws parallels between the biological and business worlds, is heavily reliant on the strategic application of ICT (see Meyer and Davis 2003).

The changes that we have seen in post-compulsory education over the latter part of the twentieth century have been enormous – reductions in funding; a significant increase in student numbers; an exponential explosion of information availability; greater knowledge and awareness of how people learn; amazing technological developments; ubiquitous access to technologies such as the Web and mobile phones; an increased number of universities; globalisation of services; and students as paying consumers. This extent of change on such a broad front makes us question whether our colleges and universities are fit for purpose any longer. Have they responded positively to the external changes with which they have been faced and, more importantly, have they made effective use of technology in their response, and as a result, are they adaptive enterprises?

There is no doubt that educational organisations have accumulated enormous amounts of technology over the years but the key question is whether this investment has been made strategically or not. How has it improved efficiency or competitive advantage, and how are we measuring any added value? The bill for technology in HE and FE over the last ten years is difficult to determine. There are indicators of high levels of spend. A Becta study on ICT and e-learning in further education published in 2004 reports that 'total numbers of computers in the 395 English Colleges [of FE] is around 320,000 – double the 1999 estimated total', and that 'the rapid growth of the sector's [FE] computer stock between 1999 and 2001 resulted in an annual net increase of around 50,000 computers a year' (Becta 2004).

In addition to this there has been a staggering growth in network availability in post-compulsory institutions as well as high levels of expenditure on administrative and learning software. Although accurate expenditure data are not available for higher education, the Universities and Colleges Information Systems Association (UCISA) annual statistics indicate that spend on ICT in HE has been above FE levels for many years. It is clear that, viewed across the whole post-compulsory sector, spending on ICT directly (on hardware, software, systems and networks) and indirectly (on training and initiative projects) runs to hundreds of millions of pounds. At this level of investment ICT should have transformed educational organisations, enabling them to adapt and ensuring continued fit with the environment in which they operate. Expectations at the outset of this journey were articulated in broad terms by the aspirations of the UK National Committee of Inquiry into Higher Education 1997, referred to as the Dearing Report, which stated that:

> the innovative exploitation of Communications and Information Technology (C&IT) holds out much promise for improving the quality, flexibility and effectiveness of higher education.
>
> (Dearing 1997)

In their response to the Dearing report UCISA said 'the successful exploitation of C&IT is pivotal to the success and health of higher education in the future' (UCISA 1997).

So how successful have we been in the exploitation of the opportunities afforded by IT? Has IT transformed processes and services in universities and colleges for the better?

A model for measuring success

To take a view on whether IT is transforming education in our colleges and universities we need to have a framework for knowing how we would know. One generic tool for measuring progress with ICT is the MIT 90s model, already outlined in the Introduction and illustrated again here in Figure 6.1.

The industry partners in the MIT 90s programme included ICL (International Computers Limited – now Fujitsu). The ICL report 'A Window on the Future' reinforced the use of ICT as a key driver of business change:

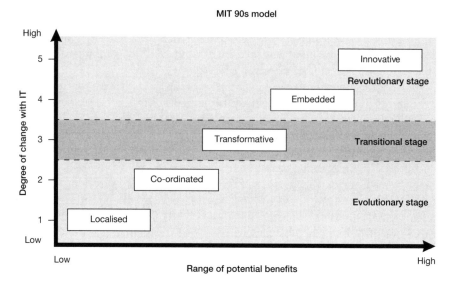

Figure 6.1 MIT 90s model of levels of technological change.
Source: adapted from Scott Morton 1991.

Organisations that have faced changes involving closely integrating IT into their business processes have achieved advantages that are not available to those who have merely applied IT to improving the efficiency of their existing processes.

(ICL 1990: 11)

The ICL report also acknowledges that organisations are groupings of people and that:

The real benefits of IT derive from the constructive combination of IT with an organisation's structure and people who are capable of exploiting the information and new functionality that IT can provide.

(1990: 11)

Herein lies a fundamental issue for education that was picked up by Sir Ron Dearing in the report on higher education mentioned above:

To help achieve this [the innovative exploitation of C&IT], we believe it will be necessary for institutions to introduce managers who have both a deep understanding of C&IT, and its application to higher education, and senior management experience. There is a shortage of such individuals within higher education. They would therefore have to be bought in or developed by institutions themselves.

(Dearing 1997)

This led to the Committee of Inquiry recommending in paragraph 42:

that all higher education institutions should develop managers who combine a deep understanding of Communications and Information Technology with senior management experience.

(Dearing 1997)

Type 42 managers, as they have since become known, remain somewhat elusive in HE and, to a lesser extent, in FE. The lack of deep understanding of the potential of ICT at senior levels in post-compulsory institutions remains partly because the route to seniority – in pre-1992 universities at least – is still through the research lab and occasionally through the class-room. Although these routes to seniority produce some excellent individuals they rarely result in a 42.

Through their professional association (UCISA) ICT managers in universities and further education colleges highlight the concern that at senior levels ICT may not have its rightful place in the strategic thinking of institutions. In the 2003 survey of the main concerns of UK HE and FE ICT managers, two of the top five issues were that:

- 'a strategic approach to developing, maintaining and upgrading the IT infrastructure needed to deliver strategic IT based academic and business services' was not being taken by institutional managers.
- managers needed to 'ensure that IT is being fully considered in the development and planning of our institutions'.

(Stinson 2004)

So where is post-compulsory education on the MIT 90s model? Has technology revolutionised these organisations? Has it been used to automate what they have always done or have they used it to do things differently, for example in the ways outlined in earlier chapters?

The 'cost' of ICT

ICT is a relatively recent 'additional cost' for universities and colleges. At the same time, 'reduction in funding' is identified as one of the forces for change acting on institutions. The arguments for spending on ICT therefore need to have considerable merit if additional funding is to be justified. Some indication was also given earlier that considerable investment has been made in ICT in general across HE and FE. As a rule of thumb institutions in general spend between 2 per cent and 5 per cent of turnover on ICT in the hope of improving their processes and services. The major areas of expenditure are on systems to support and develop business processes, and ICT for learning. Underlying these categories is a substantial expenditure on infrastructure. Although the spend is large the shopping list for ICT is enormous. Continuing rapid development of technology ensures that demands for investment continue to grow. Indeed the rate of technological change is such that expenditure has to run very fast for the institution to merely stay where it is. A clear 'investment path' emerges, driven initially by the need to maintain present provision of ICT but also by the availability of new technological 'solutions' for processes that are currently not ICT-based, or systems that enable new forms of operation. Whatever the underlying rationale there is always a case for more investment in ICT. So how has this expenditure impacted across institutional business systems, learning systems, and infrastructure?

Business systems

This 'investment path' is historically based on earlier needs to handle large volumes of data and relatively mechanistic processes. Post-compulsory organisations acquired ICT systems not to do new things but mainly to deal with the requirements of external reporting to government bodies such as HESA. Understandably, finance, HR, student records and the library were prime early candidates for computerisation. In this 'business domain' additional systems, for example those for handling alumni and marketing, have also been widely adopted by the sector. Enterprise communications have become a key part of all institutions' 'business' activity stimulating spending on email systems, collaborative software, and intranets and portals. Softer systems are now also targets for computerisation such as systems for customer relationship management and social software. Individual organisations are at different stages with each of these systems and some have systems to cover business processes not mentioned here. In order to gain a picture of where HE and FE institutions are with their ICT systems, we need to ask in general terms what an institution that is at a localised stage with its use of ICT in its business processes would look like, and how the other stages of the MIT 90s model would look for this aspect of the use of ICT (see Table 6.1).

So where are our institutions with their business systems? Over the past five years, universities and colleges have been investing in their management information systems (MIS), and working towards improving interoperability across their many legacy systems. Some have introduced managed learning environments (MLEs), combining aspects of administrative and learning support for students and staff. The Joint Information Systems Committee–funded 'Managed Learning Environments for Lifelong Learning' programme,

Table 6.1 Different levels of ICT usage in post-compulsory education, based on the MIT 90s model

Localised	Co-ordinated	Transformative	Embedded	Innovative
Organisational silos have their own system not connected to other systems	Silos have their own systems but share ICT infrastructure and data with others	Systems are regarded as owned by the whole institution and interfaced with each other	Systems are integrated and distributed access is the norm	Systems are integrated and distributed access is the norm including access by external stakeholders

for example, had the longer term strategic aim of supporting universities and colleges:

> in moving towards student-centred information systems that facilitate the mobility of the lifelong learner in the form of an individual student portal that provides a single entry point to relevant learning and administrative resources.
>
> (JISC 2004)

MLEs are about joining up systems and processes for the benefit of the learner. JISC argue that the Government e-learning and Lifelong Learning agendas mean that MLE development (regionally as well as within institutions) is a necessity. Yet they go on to note that 'some institutions are struggling to link their VLE to essential admin systems while others are a long way down the road of full integration' (JISC 2002).

Most of the pilot projects have illustrated that the UK HE and FE sectors remain at best at the co-ordinated level on the MIT 90s model; and project evaluations have often suggested that progress was undermined by varying combinations in different institutions of lack of senior management commitment or understanding, high levels of risk-aversion, 'silo' cultures, piecemeal tinkering rather than organisational re-thinking, reliance on a few enthusiastic individuals and experts rather than the wider involvement of staff and students, and a tendency to see technology as a 'neutral' solution to a problem, not as the support for strategic business and educational objectives. Clearly this is not a picture of co-ordination, and some way from a strategic approach. But the news is not all bad – some further educa-tion colleges are making significant progress with systems integration, for example Newark and Sherwood under the leadership of John Gray, which has an extensively used intranet linking all staff. There are also successes across institutions such as the Glasgow TeleColleges Network, which involves the majority of the ten FE Colleges in Glasgow in the use of shared resources. The establishment of Regional Support Centres (RSCs) funded by JISC has also served to stimulate developments in the FE sector.

Finally, and interestingly, the greatest number of, and most successful, shifts appear to be developing within the post-1992 ex-polytechnic sector, which lacks the inherent 'competitive advantage' of the pre-1992 universities. In all aspects of their work these institutions must actively compete whether it be for students or for research income. Technological innovation, and successful deployment, is viewed as key to developing 'brand identity' in these institutions. For example, Glasgow Caledonian University was an early adopter of portal technology to deliver information and services to its students and one of the first to outsource email services. In the pre-1992 sector the University of Manchester led the way in pioneering the use of ICT for delivery of student services.

Student learning systems

All UK universities and colleges now make some use of e-learning, either supported by one of the main proprietary VLE systems (Blackboard or Web-CT) or using home-grown or freeware systems. Many institutions also have a Content Management System for managing electronic documents such as Web pages. Development varies from local departmental support for e-learning enthusiasts through to an institution-wide requirement to have some aspect of all courses or modules online. Although technology can support all pedagogic models, it is usually linked to constructivist discovery approaches to learning, exemplified by Diana Laurillard in her 1993 book *Re-thinking University Teaching*. A constructivist view that understands learning as a process with communication and personal reflection at its heart requires teachers and learners to capitalise on the communications aspects of ICT, particularly in its opportunities for online conferencing, peer-group interaction, and formative assessment. These are precisely the areas where new technologies are improving opportunities and offering innovative developments (see 'Horizon Report' 2005 and 2006 from the National Media Consortium for outlines of current trends). Unfortunately, where academics are merely required to use e-learning systems, without support, the use tends to be merely as digital filing cabinet for lecture notes and handouts.

Conversely, much 'classroom ICT' also has enormous potential for preserving the status quo. Classrooms in which computer projection replaces the OHP and the electronic whiteboard replaces the blackboard hardly represent a giant leap forward in pedagogy. The traditional role of the teacher is all encompassing, as the Distributed and Electronic Learning Group (DELG) of the Learning and Skills Council point out in their report:

It is a common characteristic of 'traditional' teaching methods that the designing, planning, learning materials creation, delivery and support of a programme is all undertaken by an individual or small homogeneous group.

(LSC 2002: 22)

New communications technologies, such as blogs and wikis; digital repositories of metadata, such as students recommending to others the best sources on the teacher-issued reading; and personal development planning (pdp) that puts the ownership with, and onus on, the student, all threaten the current order as does the suggestion from DELG that:

E-learning provides opportunities to deconstruct the business of supporting learners, recognising those elements that are necessarily provided by human interaction, those that can be provided through remote provision, and those areas in which peer support has a strong part to play. Furthermore, extensive use of e-learning requires different forms of information, advice and guidance.

(LSC 2002: 22)

Such disruptive changes are unlikely to get widespread acceptance amongst an academic staff that continues to operate an education system for the benefit of the industrial machine of the twentieth century. So what might MIT 90s stages look like for the adoption and use of learning technology? As with business systems, the take-up of e-learning has been patchy, compared to the optimistic predictions of the 1990s when the Web first began to be a real force. Usage remains generally at the localised/co-ordinated level, despite the fact that Web-enabled networks are improving

Table 6.2 Learning technologies at different levels of the MIT 90s model

Localised	Co-ordinated	Transformative	Embedded	Innovative
Individual staff make use of a range of ICT resources and services to deliver their teaching	ICT used to support current practice in learning and teaching	Groups of staff use ICT to deliver new forms of student centred, active learning and supportive teaching	Widespread use of ICT to support higher order skills acquisition and learner development	Institution wide systems for learner tracking, assessment, and learner development used to support all staff and students in their learning

all the time. Individual academics and departments still resist sharing materials, sharing expertise or collaborating with others. However, as with business systems, there are examples of best practice with systems such as the virtual campus at Robert Gordon University, and by key individuals, such as the work of Gilly Salmon, formerly at the Open University and now at the University of Leicester. These build an inclusive, systematic communications network with and between students that exploits the communications aspects of technology to support personal learning, growth and development (Salmon 2003).

Infrastructure

As noted at the start of this chapter the investment in hardware, systems and networks has been considerable in most institutions across the UK. However, although many in the sector are aware of the potential and importance of systems interoperability and are committed to achieving this through open standards and service-oriented architectures, the sector is still in the very early stages of the necessary strategic impetus; and investment from senior levels is needed to make integration a reality.

This has two implications. First, universities and colleges are still struggling with the basics of getting different systems within the organisation to talk to each other and to build in robust processes of security and authentication. Not surprisingly, previous purchasing decisions have locked many in and denied them the flexibility needed to respond to changing directions of systems and standards. The costs and effort required to revise the foundation thinking on which individual departmental silos have based purchasing decisions, and to try and integrate disparate systems, is a tall order and requires revisiting fundamentals at great cost in both money and time. Second, as a consequence, post-compulsory education remains unable to take advantage of many of the possibilities offered by new technologies, both for business improvements and for a better service for students and staff.

Without an associated fundamental review – and rationalisation – of business processes, the only recourse is to use middleware as a short-term 'patch'. This approach allows for opportunistic and small-scale improvements in efficiency, but only at the co-ordinated level. The old systems thinking is not well-suited to an environment that demands a service-based approach to development as effective delivery of services cuts across the silos that own the systems. Service-based approaches demand integration, integration, integration – nothing short of a transformation, not just with technology, but also with culture and behaviour.

Of all the aspects considered so far business systems show most progress overall, in terms of engagement with issues of automation and integration.

Table 6.3 Business processes at different levels of the MIT 90s model

Localised	Co-ordinated	Transformative	Embedded	Innovative
Individual departments make use of a range of ICT systems for business processes using local data. Focus on external reporting.	Local systems with data sharing between departments. Focus on external reporting.	Functional departments become users, not owners, of organisational systems that provide access on a needs basis. Focus on external reporting and internal monitoring.	Systems owned and run by the organisation with use owned and managed locally – no data duplication. Focus on external reporting, internal monitoring, forecasting and improvement.	Access based on information and service needs to a menu of (Web) services. Focus as previous plus an emphasis on service.

There is a widespread acknowledgement that joined-up systems and use of data in planning and strategic decision-making is vital to success. However, although many UK institutions might feel that they are on the brink of transformation, few have achieved this. Good international examples are Queensland University of Technology (QUT) and the University of California, Los Angeles (UCLA). QUT have integrated administrative ICT with student services by developing and then integrating 'best of breed' technology that suits particular needs with the organisation rather than, for example, an enterprise resource planning system from one manufacturer.

UCLA began using electronic data exchange (EDI) for invoices in the 1990s and adopted a strategy to Web-enable all their major transactional legacy systems in 1998. The student self-service Web application URSA[1] delivers virtual student services via the MyUCLA Web portal[2] which, in turn, is backed by an e-procurement system, virtual human resource management, virtual organisational performance and reporting management and a business portal (UC2010 2000).

If, then, this is a summary of the existing state of play of business systems, learning systems and infrastructures within universities and colleges; what is the current situation in relation to those other aspects focused on by e-business, customer focus and organisational integration? Lets look at these in turn.

'Customer focus' and the student experience

The relationship of the student to the institution isn't what it used to be. It is relatively common now to regard students as customers, although this is more accepted in post-1992 institutions and colleges and by the professional support side of institutions rather than by the academic staff. However, the concept of customer in HE and FE doesn't quite work – even in e-businesses there is a shift away from simple buy/sell transactions to a long term 'relationship'. Like customers students can complain but, as with other service industries, they can't bring 'the product' back. They are deeply personally involved in 'the product'. It is their life and cannot be wound back in response to errors or unsatisfactory experiences. Perhaps a more robust concept of the relationship between the student and the organisation is that of member. (See also Chapter 4.) Students are truly members of educational organisations. They share in the development of the organisation, in the design of its services, and through consumption and dialogue in the evaluation of the organisation. Not only are students members of the organisation, many more of them are now also set to be paying members. Although students under 19 in FE will still receive their education free (and most mature and part-time students in HE and FE have always had to pay), full-time HE students in England are now responsible for their own fees. Students in Scotland who pay in arrears are probably less likely to focus on the value for money aspect of what they receive – in England fees are a focus change in the student/organisation relationship. Clearly where ICT can be used to enhance the paying student's experience and improve the quality of their education, then it should be.

Many twenty-first century students are busy people who have to balance the demand of a full-time education with a job and/or a family. The scarce resource from their perspective is time. The use of ICT for the delivery of advice, guidance, counselling and learner support is relatively uncharted territory for most institutions but does present a real opportunity to make use of systems to focus and integrate services – and save time for students. Most institutions have a Web presence for these services, and some of these are extensive, but they rarely provide anything beyond information support. The extension of such services to automate the mundane is an essential, albeit basic, application of ICT for all institutions. As noted in the e-learning section above there is a particular need for rethinking student support: 'furthermore, extensive use of e-learning requires different forms of information, advice, and guidance' (LSC 2002). The provision of services to students in the five stages of the MIT 90s model might look something like the representation in Table 6.4.

Students are already becoming fluent in a variety of communication modes, and are increasingly likely to have at least a mobile phone or a PDA, if not a PC. At a Glasgow Caledonian University's freshers' address some years ago when asked who has access to a PC over 80 per cent of the audience

Table 6.4 Student focus at different levels of the MIT 90s model

Localised	Co-ordinated	Transformative	Embedded	Innovative
Individual services such as careers and counselling make some use of ICT systems for own record keeping, bookings, and tracking	Web based information support provided for information on student services and appointment booking	Students have access to information and transaction services online	All student support services integrated within a student experience environment	Student experience environment extends to integration business and learning systems and provides access to information and transactions with staff trained to deliver in depth specialist support

responded positively; when asked about a mobile phone the response was 100 per cent. Students are no strangers to technology and portable devices are now flying off the shelves much faster than desktop machines. More than any other area 'customer' focus is demand, rather than supply, driven and universities and colleges need to make urgent efforts to respond to this demand. Post-compulsory institutions in the UK are well placed to respond to this demand being at the 'transformative' stage on the MIT 90s model. Examples of best practice, however, are not to be found in the UK but in the US. For instance, Penn State University (which began correspondence study programmes in 1892) launched the World Campus in 1998, with a fully integrated set of student services.[3] As already mentioned in Chapter 4 the University of Phoenix also puts student services at the centre of its distance learning provision. The for-profit organisations such as UNext and NextEd are explicitly competing in terms of the quality of service the student receives, as in NextEd's 'Total Student Experience' model – 'a thinking framework for considering the whole system a student interacts with, including educational, commercial and societal components, when they enter a course of study' (Cox 2001).

Towards the integrated organisation

In the early 1990s UK universities and polytechnics were denied ICT funding unless they had an ICT strategy. This familiar way of stimulating strategy production in institutions has also been used in FE and for the late-1990s push for information strategies. Although the production of an information strategy, ICT strategy, ICT policy (and all its constituent rules and regulations to 'control' the behaviour of users, control viruses, ensure standards, and preserve security), is important, it is even more important that it is implemented. As the use of ICT has grown in our HE and FE institutions then the need for more policies and strategies has emerged. The Internet requires a Web strategy; new legislation a data protection and freedom of information strategy; and the growing mountain of information a records management strategy. Beyond production and implementation, however, lies integration. If the policies and strategies relating to information and communications technology are not developed from a business need and not integrated with business activities then they are merely self-serving. The strategy should integrate with, and serve to integrate, the business. On the MIT 90s model policy levels might be that shown in Table 6.5.

Conclusion

Integrating ICT into business processes has the potential to spawn new models and relationships. As mentioned at the outset of this chapter our current organisational silos are a major barrier to transformation. For the user, however, these silos are meaningless and at best add nothing to, and at worst detract from, clarity and simplicity of service provision. Students should not have to understand how the university or college is structured in order to access its services, nor indeed should they have to understand the nuances of HE and FE in order to progress their education.

This means that at the innovative end of the MIT 90s model we should be using ICT to demystify our complex organisations and structures. There is a sense in which structural reorganisation is irrelevant. To the user what is important is service integration. This can be achieved in two ways: by restructuring the people or by co-ordinating their services from the student's

Table 6.5 Policy at different levels of the MIT 90s model

Localised	Co-ordinated	Transformative	Embedded	Innovative
Strategy and policy formulated and implemented at local departmental level	Local policy and strategy sits within an overall institutional framework	Strategy and policy focused on organisational business needs	ICT acknowledged in, and drives, overall business strategy	ICT components of business strategy stimulate new business relationships and models

point of view using ICT. For most organisations and members of staff the second is more palatable and can produce good results for the user. It is, however, not staff neutral as it does require openness, transparency and unselfish sharing of processes, data, information and knowledge. ICT also offers the opportunity to share between organisations such as the 'follow the sun' provision of 24 × 7 × 365 help desk support that some UK and Australian Universities have experimented with. Taking a service approach to our provision also tempts us to consider outsourcing non-vital systems such as email, VLE provision, and major operational systems such as finance, HR, and student records. The power and flexibility of ICT is such that the possibilities are endless – the only barrier is the human infrastructure and its associated culture.

Much of this chapter has illustrated what universities and colleges are *not* doing. These are opportunities that are being missed. Although it cannot be expected that every UK university and college will somehow transform itself into an e-business overnight (especially given the recent history of false assumptions about how quickly e-learning would replace conventional education), we suggest that post-compulsory educational institutions should focus on their 'whole business' and learn from the ways e-business has integrated new technologies with its strategic objectives, organisational frameworks and service provision. The rest of this book is taken up with exploring how a UK university or college can 'get from here to there' in designing and implementing the necessary changes.

Notes

1   See UCLA website www.ursa.ucla.edu.
2   See UCLA website www.my.ucla.edu.
3   See Penn State University website www.worldcampus.psu.edu/wc/Student Services.shtml.

Bibliography

Becta (August 2004) 'ICT and e-learning in further education: embedded technology, evolving practice'. Online. Available at http://ferl.becta.org.uk/display.cfm?res ID=7894 (accessed December 2006).

Cox, Geoffrey (2001) 'UNEXT: innovator or barbarian?' *University Teaching as E-Business? Research and Policy Agendas*, pp. 55–59. Center for Studies in Higher Education (CSHE) University of California, Berkeley. Online. Available at www.cshe.berkeley.edu/publications/papers/papers/elearning.pdf (accessed January 2004).

Dearing, R. (1997) *The Dearing Report on Higher Education in the Learning Society*, National Committee of Inquiry into Higher Education.

International Computer Ltd (ICL) (1990) 'A window on the future: an ICL briefing for management on the findings of the management in the 1990's research programme'.

JISC (2002) 'Managed learning environments, joined up systems and the problems of organisational change', author Jos Boys, March. Online. Available at www.jisc.ac.uk (accessed January 2003).

JISC (2004) 'Managed learning environments for lifelong learning', Bristol. Online. Available at www.jisc.ac.uk/whatwedo/programmes/programme_buildmle_hefe.aspx (accessed December 2006).

Laurillard, Diana (1993) *Rethinking University Teaching: a framework for the effective use of educational technology*. London: Routledge.

Learning Skills Council (LSC) Distributed and Electronic Learning Group (DELG), (2002) Online. Available at http://readingroom.lsc.gov.uk/pre2005/learning opportunities/ict/delg-report.pdf (accessed December 2006).

Meyer, C. and Davis, S. (2003) *It's Alive: the coming convergence of information, biology and business*. New York: Crown Business.

National Media Consortium (NMC) (2005) 'Horizon report', joint publication of the NMC and the National Learning Infrastructure Initiative (NLII), an EDUCAUSE program, ISBN 0–9765087–0-2. Online. Available at www.nmc.net/pdf/2005_Horizon_Report.pdf (accessed December 2006).

National Media Consortium (NMC) (2006) 'Horizon report'. Online. Available at www.nmc.org/horizon (accessed 1 October 2007).

Salmon, Gilly (2003) *E-Moderating: the key to teaching and learning online*, 2nd edn, London: Routledge Farmer.

Stinson, I. (2004) 'UCISA top concerns process 2003–4: importance to the UCISA Community'. Online. Available at www.ucisa.ac.uk/activities/surveys/tc/2004/survey-results.html (accessed December 2006).

UC2010 (2000) 'A new business architecture for the University of California'. Online. Available at http://uc2010.ucsd.edu/pdf/uc2010final.pdf (accessed December 2006).

UCISA's response to Dearing (1997) approach to Communications and Information Technology (C&IT). Online. Available at www.ucisa.ac.uk/about/marketing/pr/pr6.htm (accessed December 2006).

Chapter 7

Getting from here to there

Strategies for change

David Nicol and Michael Coen

In the previous chapters some of the major drivers for change in the application of ICT to the post-compulsory education sector have been examined. These chapters also explored the opportunities afforded by ICT to benefit the processes and services delivered by universities and colleges. In addition, the last chapter suggested the MIT 90s model as a tool to evaluate institutional progress in the use of ICT. It used the model to identify five phases of success from localised applications of ICT through to the high-level integration of ICT across all institutional processes. This model could be used to describe in broad terms what progress the institution has made in a variety of areas: in relation to ICT system integration; with reference to the application of technology to teaching and learning; in terms of customer focus; and in relation to supporting organisational integration.

This chapter examines how one might approach the management of change in the institutional uses of ICT. It builds on the analysis in the previous chapter by considering how institutions might plan their move from their current position to where they want to be. Although change in the use of technology is inevitable and cannot be resisted (given the external drivers outlined in previous chapters), an informed approach to change will place the institution in a much stronger position in the increasingly competitive world of post-compulsory education. The challenge for institutions is to create a situation where changes using ICT can be implemented to the maximum benefit in terms of strategic priorities but with the lowest risk and cost (Ford *et al.* 1996). This requires not only change-management strategies but also methodologies for making sound investment decisions and tools to monitor and evaluate the benefits of changes resulting from these decisions.

Change management processes in post-compulsory institutions

The starting point for any major institutional change involves knowing where the institution is going. In universities and colleges, direction is normally defined within vision or mission statements, in educational and business objectives and in operational strategies and policies. According to Ford *et al.*, institutional vision 'needs to embrace not only the services [the institution] intends to enable and provide, how and to whom it intends to provide them, but also the principles and values it intends to support and demonstrate' (1996: 20). Also, importantly, the vision and objectives must be shared and owned across the institution. Planning for change in the use of technologies in universities and colleges is, however, complicated by a number of factors.

First, there are problems with the extent to which the institutional visions are translated into business strategies, expressed as objectives and critical success factors. For example, Coen *et al.* (2004) explored the reasons given for ICT use in teaching and learning across a range of HE and FE institutions within the UK. The following is a list of reasons given in strategy documents and by staff in discussion (Nicol 2004):

- to improve learning quality;
- to improve the student experience;
- to reduce costs;
- to gain competitive advantage;
- to expand or break into new markets;
- to widen access;
- to facilitate flexible learning;
- to improve retention;
- to improve organisational efficiency.

What is notable about this list is that most institutions tended to identify the same general, and broad, objectives for the educational uses of ICT and only in a few instances were these objectives described in a way that might help institutions target a specific market segment. In addition, few institutions had actually prioritised these objectives or were actively using them as a yardstick against which to measure the effectiveness of ICT innovations. Although the above list was provided in relation to the educational uses of ICT, similar generalised lists are often provided for administrative uses of ICT: for example, to produce more effective management systems, to enhance the exchange of information with external agencies (e.g. UCAS, banks, libraries, suppliers, etc.), to replace obsolete legacy systems, or to comply with legislation.

A second issue in managing change in post-compulsory education is that different stakeholders (registry, academic, IT services, administrative, finance and support staff) have different perspectives on priorities and they rarely have a chance to share their ideas and concerns with others. This leads to lack of consensus about the issues, difficulties and priorities for change. A third, and related, point is that costly ICT applications (e.g. the purchase of a virtual learning environment (VLE) or a new administrative system) tend to have repercussions across the whole institution with the result that it is difficult to address issues of change in isolation. For example, the application of new technologies is blurring traditional role boundaries and responsibilities while at the same time it is requiring much greater collaboration than in the past by staff in academic departments with those in support and administrative departments. As many writers have noted, the real difficulties in managing change in the use of ICT are human, social and cultural, not technological.

A fourth consideration is that educational institutions have different trajectories for change based on their history, student market and culture. In some institutions, change is driven more from the top (top-down), with senior managers setting strategy resulting in an inter-related set of ICT projects implemented lower down in faculties and departments. In other institutions, the culture is more bottom-up, with ICT projects initiated by staff locally, for example, in departments with projects scaled up to institutional level if they are successful. Although, a dual approach to change is recommended in educational organisations, with top-down and bottom-up issues addressed concurrently (Fullan 1993; Trowler *et al.* 2003), these trajectory differences do suggest that there might be variations in how change is managed in different institutional types. A related point is that different types of ICT applications might also be implemented in different ways. A finance system is likely to result in a more top-down implementation trajectory than a VLE.

This chapter presents two sets of tools that might help institutions plan, manage and evaluate change. The next section describes tools and methodologies that might help institutions formulate their strategies for the use of ICT, refine existing strategies or identify risks associated with strategies. The subsequent section identifies how institutions might make investment decisions and monitor and evaluate the effects of these decisions. In both sections the change examples used refer to the application of ICT in teaching and learning. However, it should be noted that the frameworks, models, methods and principles discussed are equally appropriate to applications in other areas of institutional functioning (e.g. research or administrative systems) and processes.

Managing strategic change

Creating a clearer blueprint about reasons for ICT use within colleges and universities is a first step in change management. Moreover, this step is vital when the purpose is to enable educational institutions to make concrete choices among competing investments. Nicol and Coen (2004) have developed a methodology and associated tools to help educational institutions develop their strategies for ICT, review them or implement them. The methodology draws on a framework for strategic change originally proposed by Scott Morton (1991). The framework presented in Figure 7.1 was developed for use within the business sector. Applied to post-compulsory education, it shows an institution's effectiveness in the use of ICT as being a function of six inter-related and inter-dependent elements:

- the external environment within which the institution is operating;
- the institutional strategy (or strategies) in relation to ICT;
- the way human resources (HR) are prepared and deployed to support the implementation of ICT (individuals and their roles);
- the organisational structures that support the application of ICT;
- the characteristics of the technology being applied;
- the management processes that support the implementation, cultural embedding and evaluation of ICT applications.

A number of basic assumptions underlie the use of the framework for strategic change. First, it is assumed that the management of change is

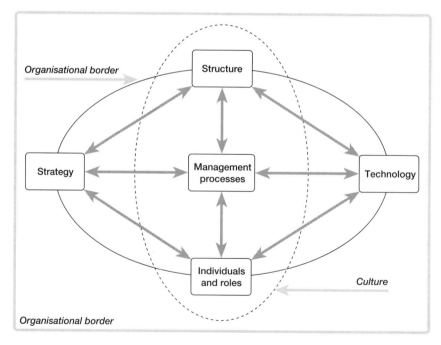

Figure 7.1 Framework for strategic change.
Source: Scott Morton 1991.

about managing the interaction of the elements (strategy, structure, management processes, etc.) and their configurations rather than just about managing the elements themselves. A second assumption is that where the elements are integrated (i.e. there is a goodness of fit) and all pulling in the same direction then ICT implementations are more likely to be embedded in the institution and risk more effectively managed. Third, the fit between internal configuration and the external environment is important in change management. For example, the success of an educational institution will depend partly on its ability to provide products to meet market needs. Fourth, the framework assumes that cultural issues (structure, management processes and individuals/roles) mediate the strategy–technology relationship and that the cultural axis of the framework will be more important for some types of ICT implementations (e.g. a VLE implementation versus a payroll system). Finally, the framework makes no assumptions about the trajectories of institutional change; change could be driven from any of the elements (from changes in staff roles or from managers setting strategy). However, it does assume that bottom-up and top-down processes interact regardless of institutional type.

Nicol and Coen have used this framework in work with universities and colleges as a tool to help stakeholders formulate or develop their e-learning strategy, and to help stakeholders identify the risks associated with an already formulated e-learning strategy. The basic methodology has been piloted across a range of institutions (two FE colleges, a pre-1992 and post-1992 university and within a Russell-group university). It involves bringing together staff from across all areas of institutional functioning (management, HR, finance, teaching, library, IT services, support services, etc.) to work together in small cross-functional groups to discuss and identify issues (risk or strategy) under each of the six headings (elements). The actual steps of an all-day workshop implemented in one university are described in Box 7.1. The purpose of this workshop was to help the institution refine its e-learning strategy, to identify the risks associated with the strategy and to identify ways of addressing those risks.[1]

The following are some of the findings recorded when the framework and approach was used in post-compulsory institutional settings. First, participants gained a clearer idea about why the institution was engaging in ICT-supported activities and what these activities were. Second, bringing staff together from different functional areas with different perspectives resulted in a greater sense of ownership and agreement about priorities for the future. Third, the process proved highly effective in uncovering a wide range of interrelated issues across the whole of the institution, and especially social and cultural issues and barriers to the use of ICT in teaching and learning. In addition, senior managers gained a greater understanding of the concerns of staff about the use of ICT in teaching and learning.

Box 7.1 Using the strategic change model to clarify institutional direction: a workshop example

Step 1: Identify a facilitator or facilitators

A facilitator (or facilitators) approved by senior management is required to co-ordinate the use of the change management model during a consultation workshop or series of workshops. In this example, facilitators from another institution ran the workshop.

Step 2: Identify the key stakeholders

An internal member of staff must identify appropriate representatives from across the institution to participate in the workshop. The aim is to gather as wide a range of views as possible, including the views of sceptics. For example, discussion about e-learning strategy issues would normally include senior managers, academic practitioners, representatives from relevant administrative and support areas and perhaps other stakeholders (e.g. students).

Step 3: Plan the workshop

Different workshops are possible. The intention of the example described here was to help the institution to clarify its strategic objectives for e-learning and to identify the risks/issues associated with those objectives and ways of addressing these risks.

Step 4: Run the workshop

The format for the all-day workshop was as follows:

(i)   The Pro-Vice Chancellor for Learning and Teaching and the Pro-Vice Chancellor for Strategic Systems Development presented current strategic imperatives for e-learning and emphasised the importance of the workshop;

(ii) Participants working in cross-functional groups were asked to identify current developments in e-learning within the institution;

(iii) The same cross-functional groups were then asked to identify up to five strategic benefits of e-learning for the institution and to rank/prioritise these benefits using their own criteria;

(iv) In the afternoon each participant (individual reflection without discussion) filled out a pro-forma that asked them to note down what they thought were the issues and barriers to strategy implementation using the headings of the framework for strategic change (i.e. external drivers, strategy, structure, individuals/roles, management processes and technology), and for each barrier to make a recommendation that would help overcome it.

(v) The cross-functional groups then worked together to discuss the issues and barriers they had identified in (iv) and to create a group report.

In (ii), (iii) and (v), there was a plenary report-back session after the group discussion. This allowed developments, strategic priorities, issues raised and recommendations to be publicised, and drawn together, in open discussion by the facilitators.

Step 5: Report and follow-up activities
The workshop ended with a clear indication from a senior manager of how the outputs will be fed into future planning processes. The external facilitators compiled a report on the day for senior management.

Importantly, the procedures described above must be followed through after the workshop if the goal is to formalise, prioritise and operationalise strategic objectives. Although cross-functional groups tend to produce similar sets of overlapping issues, each group tends to have its own perspective and priorities. The facilitators help to bring ideas together during the workshop and in the post-workshop written report. Indeed, this report draws on a rich data set including individual reflective reports, group reports and flipchart records from the plenary discussions. However, senior managers must ultimately take ownership of this information by discussing the findings in relevant strategy committees and by using the information collated to inform action planning and implementation. These processes might also lead to further consultation and discussion across the institution and to further input to management thinking. This is consistent with the framework for change management presented, which envisages that the process is iterative and that cycles of top-down and bottom-up processes are required to ensure buy-in and ownership.

Overall, the outcomes of the consultative workshop described here were greater clarity about the vision and objectives for ICT use in the institution, the identification of priorities and a range of issues that must be addressed both in the short and long term and some suggestions about how these might be addressed. These workshop processes have the potential to help senior managers clarify strategic objectives and to target where subsequent investments might yield maximum return and where more research is required.

Evaluating the costs and benefits of technology implementation: making investment choices

In the previous section a framework and methodology were presented that could be used to help an institution to formulate or refine its strategy for the application of ICT. In this section the concern is with how institutions might ensure that they obtain the best value from their investment choices in relation to strategy. There are three key requirements to making effective investment decisions:

- alignment of investment decisions with strategic objectives in the institution;
- formal methodologies for evaluating the costs and benefits of investments;
- better procedures for evaluating the risks associated with investments.

In some cases practices can be adopted from business and industry (see Chapter 3), but due to the distinctive funding processes, culture and organisation of post-compulsory education, in many cases, new and innovative approaches will have to be developed from within the education sector itself.

Evaluation issues

Research indicates that current procedures for making investment decisions about, and for evaluating the benefits of, ICT use in post-compulsory institutions are under-developed (Nicol and Coen 2003a, 2003b). This is especially true in areas where the benefits from applications are soft, cut across the institution and are therefore difficult to measure (e.g. implementation of an institutional repository or a VLE) and where there are many people within the institution who have a stake in the decision-making process (e.g. ICT services, teachers, administrators, support staff). Even in areas where ICT applications have a narrower range of influence and are amenable to quantitative outputs (e.g. evaluation of the implications of a new finance system), some still argue that evaluations are not as rigorous and as systematic as in the business sector.

Most evaluations of the use of ICT applications in universities and in colleges are conducted at a local (departmental) rather than at a strategic level. Teachers or researchers are involved in evaluating the educational benefits deriving from ICT implementations in teaching and learning. Administrative personnel might evaluate the choice of ICT systems based on an analysis of cost versus features (functions) without necessarily taking into account the wider human factors surrounding actual use. ICT investments should be evaluated from the wider strategic perspective; for example, identifying the value that an ICT initiative in teaching might have on organisational and on community objectives.

ICT implementations in post-compulsory education are often expensive (e.g. digital repositories, VLEs, student records systems) and, in the current climate of resource constraints, institutional managers must make critical decisions about what to invest in. However, funding bodies are becoming increasingly concerned that post-compulsory institutions do not have systematic procedures or appropriate tools to make informed decisions about complex ICT investments. From the perspective of senior managers:

- investment decisions about ICT projects must be aligned to institutional strategies (i.e. investments that progress institutional strategies are more attractive than those that do not);
- choice of ICT applications must be evaluated against a wide range of strategic objectives (e.g. organisational, educational and community objectives) rather than against a narrow spectrum of objectives (e.g. student satisfaction, efficiency of information flow);
- value, not just costs, critically influences investment decisions;
- sustainability of the initiative, beyond the initial funding, must be considered.

What is needed to address these requirements is some kind of cost–benefit analysis (CBA) linked to institutional strategy. This would help those in the institution decide whether, for example, investing in a new VLE or in laptops for students or a new finance or student records system was best value for money. But why is the use of CBA not as common in post-compulsory education as it is in industry? There are at least three reasons. First, it is difficult to get agreement internally (across different institutional stakeholders) about which benefits criteria (in relation to strategic plans) should be used to evaluate investment options and in agreeing what would count as evaluative evidence. Second, there are problems in reconciling different types of evidence and methodologies (quantitative costing versus qualitative benefits evaluation) including the fact that those with expertise in costing rarely work alongside those with expertise in benefits evaluation. Third, finance systems in the post-compulsory education sector are not geared to producing costing information that might aid investment comparisons (e.g. information that would allow one to identify and apportion costs to value-adding activities). There are also cultural barriers to costing (e.g. especially in relation to staff time), although this is changing with the introduction of full economic costing for research activities.

The insight cost–benefit analysis model

Nicol and Coen have proposed a CBA model to support investment decisions in ICT at institutional level (Nicol and Coen 2003a, 2003b). Like the strategy model above, it has been used in relation to ICT applications in teaching and learning but it has wider applications. The Insight CBA model is intended to help senior managers make investment decisions in a more systematic way. The model has been piloted in five institutions – a pre-1992 and post-1992 university, an FE college and sixth form college and within a federated institution. A key assumption underlying the Insight model is that decision-makers rely as much on qualitative information (about impact of benefits) as on quantitative cost information to inform their reasoning. Box 7.2 identifies the steps of CBA that are supported by the model.

Like the strategic change process described above, the Insight model is highly dependent on negotiation and dialogue. Teachers might consider some areas more strategically important than would the finance or IT director. This indicates the need for managers to involve key stakeholders from different areas of institutional functioning in discussions at the outset when agreeing the criteria for evaluation. Similarly, a common problem after an evaluation is that the evaluator comes back with the results and is told that the methods used were inappropriate (see Patton 1977). This can be avoided by making sure that the decision-making group not only agrees the benefits criteria beforehand but also discusses and agrees the evaluation methods. Cost–benefit analysis in post-compulsory education is not a mechanical process, rather it is educative. Undertaking the 'journey' that the evaluation proposes is as valuable, if not more valuable, than the getting to the final destination (the output ratio of the cost–benefit analysis). Senior managers have been making intuitive decisions for years about what to invest in. The value of the CBA model and the methodology for use is that they ensure that decision making is more systematic, rigorous and transparent than it has been in the past.

The Insight model and steps can be carried out both to support options appraisal after an ICT implementation and to help make investment decisions before implementation. The advantage of retrospective evaluation is that it is possible to collect harder evidence of costs and benefits. If the appraisal were carried out prior to the start of a new investment (e.g. to make an investment decision) then the cost–benefits data in the model would necessarily be more provisional and subjective. Also in this situation, predictive analysis would benefit significantly from an assessment of the risks associated with different ICT investment options. In that case, the procedures identified in the first half of this chapter to identify the risks associated with strategic change could be applied.

The Insight model described here was devised to help decision-makers evaluate choices regarding ICT investments. Key features of the model are that it can be adapted to different organisational structures, that it concentrates on high-level costs, that it takes an institution-wide perspective on benefits, and that it focuses decision making on strategic priorities,

Box 7.2 Application of the Insight CBA model

Step 1: Form a decision-making group
Identify the key stakeholders involved in making decisions about ICT investment options and form a decision-making group.

Step 2: Define the parameters of the decision
Explicitly define the parameters of the decision – is it a comparison of existing pilots or projects based on historic data, an appraisal of future options based on forecast data or an invest/don't invest comparison?

Step 3: Clarify benefits against which options will be evaluated and determine their weightings
Work with the decision-making group to (i) agree between 3–7 benefits criteria – those that matter most to the institution and that would be used to evaluate the options. In other words, these criteria should be aligned with the institution's wider strategic objectives and, where appropriate, should go beyond localised benefits. (ii) Agree the weightings for each criteria and the methodology for the evaluation of benefits.

Step 4: Gather cost and benefits data
Cost information is collected using a modification of activity based costing. This uses high-level cost data focusing on relative cost changes brought about by the innovation. Benefits information is collated in relation to the agreed categories with each option rated against that category.

Step 5: Produce outputs and discuss changes in criteria weightings
Produce the outputs – a cost–benefit analysis for each investment option. At this point it is vital that there is further discussion with the decision-making group to explore possible effects of changes in the benefits weightings and ratings. Dialogue is essential.

those that matter most to the institution. The value of the model and the methodology for its use is that they ensure that decision making is more systematic, rigorous and transparent than it has been in the past. A detailed discussion of the Insight model in relation to its application to ICT initiatives in teaching and learning is available in Draper (2003: 118–21) and Nicol and Coen (2003a, 2003b).

Conclusion

In the current climate of resource constraints there is considerable pressure on post-compulsory educational institutions to put in place procedures to support strategic planning for new applications of ICT and for risk assessment of these investments. If used appropriately, the framework for strategic change and the methodology described in the first half of this chapter should help to ensure that change is a consultative and institution-wide process. Indeed, it should help institutions to avoid situations, for example, where they install highly innovative technologies but fail to provide sufficient training to support their use, or situations where the strategy for ICT use has strong buy-in but where extant organisational structures hamper implementation.

Coen, *et al.* (2005) carried out a survey within the HE sector to investigate whether institutions used CBA and what framework was being used. The findings revealed that although CBA was widely used, few, if any, institutions applied a structured framework involving key stakeholders (involving the actual users of systems) to inform their investment decisions. The Insight CBA model should help address this gap. Indeed, the application of CBA will become more important now that the HE and FE funding councils in the UK are rolling out directives that all research and external activities should be fully costed (full economic costing).

In conclusion, ICT is profoundly influencing the core business of the post-compulsory education sector. Senior managers are not only tasked with making sense of these complex and at times contradictory influences, but also with providing leadership in relation to the direction of change. However, productive change also requires that those working in educational institutions not only feel positive about the adoption of technology but also have some ownership over the change agenda. This chapter has provided a framework, a model and associated processes that can be used to enhance ownership and engagement in change. Both the framework and the model assume that creative solutions to change arise out of discussion, negotiation and interaction and that cultural and social issues are paramount. They also assume that some structure is necessary to facilitate change but that too much structure might be inhibiting (Stacey, 1996). Hence, the chapter ends by recommending not that institutions *adopt* these tools and processes rigidly but that stakeholders *adapt* them to fit their own institutional type and context.

Note

1   For more details about the processes, including alternative workshop plans, worksheets, exemplar presentations and a management briefing paper, see www.insight.strath.ac.uk/projects/risk/index.htm.

Bibliography

Bates, A.W. (2000) *Managing Technological Change: strategies for college and university leaders*. San Francisco, CA: Jossey-Bass.

Coen, M., Breslin, C., Nicol, D.J., and Howell, D. (2004) 'Risk management of e-learning: a JISC-funded project'. Online. Available at www.insight.strath.ac.uk/projects/risk/index.htm (accessed 1 December 2006).

Coen, M., Kelly, U. and Breslin, C. (2005) 'Information systems management and governance: a JISC-funded project'. Online. Available at www.insight.strath.ac.uk/projects/itgov/index.htm (accessed 1 December 2006).

Draper, S. (2003) 'The importance of cost–benefit analysis: a response', *Association for Learning Technology Journal* 11(3): 118–21.

Ford, P. *et al.* (1996) *Managing Change in Higher Education*. Buckingham, UK: The Society for Research in Higher Education and the Open University Press.

Fullan, M. (1993) *Change Forces: probing the depths of educational reform*. London and New York: The Falmer Press.

Nicol, D.J. and Coen, M. (2003a) 'A model for evaluating the institutional costs and benefits of ICT initiatives in teaching and learning in higher education', *Association for Learning Technology Journal* 11(2): 46–60.

Nicol, D.J. and Coen, M. (2003b) 'The importance of cost–benefit analysis: a response', *Association for Learning Technology Journal* 11(3): 122–4.

Nicol, D. and Coen, M. (2004) 'The risks associated with e-learning investments in FE and HE'. Senior Management Briefing Paper. Prepared for JISC. Online. Available at www.insight.strath.ac.uk/projects/risk/documents/briefing_paper.pdf.

Patton, M. (1997) *Utilisation-focused Evaluation*. London: Sage.

Scott Morton, M.S. (1991) *The Corporation of the 1990s: information technology and organisational transformation*. New York: Oxford University Press.

Stacey, R. (1996) *Complexity and Creativity in Organizations*. San-Francisco, CA: Berrett-Koehler.

Trowler, P., Saunders, M. and Knight, P. (2003) 'Change thinking, change practices'. The Learning and Teaching Support Network Generic Centre, UK. Online. Available at www.heacademy.ac.uk/resources.asp?process=full_record&section=generic&id=262 (accessed 1 December 2006).

Chapter 8

Getting from here to there

Improving processes and adding value

Daxa Patel, John Powell and Jos Boys

Chapter 6 presented an analysis of where current institutions are in their integration of ICT into institutional culture. This chapter suggests that in order to move from co-ordinated use towards a more transformational use – that is, part or whole institutional redesign – we need to do two things. First, we should make explicit the core and secondary processes of our institutions in a post-compulsory educational context; and, second, we need to understand and then exploit the potential offered by e-enabled services to improve educational provision.

How, then, might current UK HE and FE institutions more effectively take forward the transformation of what they currently do, and learn from the mistakes of the past? Over the last 20 years many businesses have gone down the process re-engineering route, taking on board Hammer's phrase 'don't automate, obliterate' (Hammer 1990: 104–12) and totally redesigned their processes. As Chapter 3 has shown, this was to take advantage of new opportunities offered by information and communication technology – specifically, its ability to connect people who are geographically spread and to share data and information in different ways. Cisco, for example, have redefined their core business as selling network technology (which is as much about handling customer relations as the nuts and bolts of manufacturing network hardware). Universities and colleges in the UK have built up many areas of good practice within their institutions, but still tend to rely on unwieldy processes, developed and improved piecemeal and underpinned by a long history of departmental or functional autonomy. This can make it hard for universities and colleges to have a detailed overview of the full range of processes taking place at any one time. The first stage is therefore to map what already exists:

> fact finding will invariably involve carrying out audits and mapping exercises. For example you might do audits of the functions and processes in different departments and then a mapping exercise of where they connect or overlap and identify potential gaps and how this information relates to the proposed MLE project. Audits might also focus

on providing an outline of existing organisational structures and the mapping of existing practices. A major difficulty with this is making the tacit explicit, as much of the information resides with individuals rather than being formally recorded. To take the example of the lifecycle of the student recruitment: people involved in the activity will have multiple and overlapping roles and functions, processes will be carried out in different ways under different circumstances, the process is unlikely to be clear cut or linear, and is likely to include redundant and repetitive actions. Finally much of the knowledge and understanding of the process will be in the minds of those involved in the process, not recorded in any way. This will be drawn on almost intuitively with decisions being made based on past experience and local understanding.

(JISC 2005)

There are, of course, many different process review methods for first analysing existing processes and then redesigning them, which incorporate a variety of approaches to the management of change. Here the aim is only to show some of the ways in which what a university or college does can be articulated more clearly. In the 1990s, for example, one UK university first undertook a scoping study of all its existing processes. Figure 8.1 was created as one of the outcomes from the scoping study. It is offered here as an example of how an educational institution might define its core processes (in this case divided into five). The diagram is not offered as a correct 'solution', only as an example of how core processes might be described. Each institution will have a different take (although Hammer (1990) argues that no organisation should have more than eight core processes).

This university's review team then focused on one process in particular – student entry – itself understood as a sub-component of the core process called 'managing the student experience'. Their student entry process was then defined as 'a comprehensive and continuous process designed to help the University achieve and maintain the optimum recruitment and retention rates of students.' In redesign terms, the process was seen as starting as soon as a potential student became aware of the university and only ended at the point where they became fully established as a student. Within these boundaries, five supporting sub-processes were identified – 'attract applicants'; 'process enquiries'; 'process applications'; 'register students'; and 'orientate students'. These processes were conceived of as parallel rather than sequential processes and continuous, developmental processes rather than 'events', and also as highly interdependent.

This mapping process was undertaken through a series of consultations with key stakeholders. A process of sharing – and crucially agreeing – the sequence and content of the core processes revealed to key stakeholders the gaps and duplications that were occurring. Differences in opinion about what was important (or even, over what was actually happening or

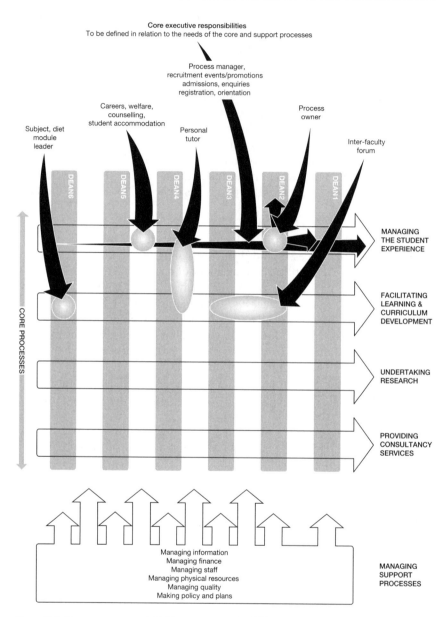

Figure 8.1 Core processes definitions as part of a UK university's process review exercise.

intended) could be argued out. Moreover, stakeholders were able to see ways of improving the whole sequence of events from the applicant/student point of view.

This mapping exercise was complex and required many discussion meetings with different groupings across the university before a commonly agreed and validated understanding of processes could be articulated. Such a process redesign method is one example of ways of developing and changing institutions (see Chapter 7). The JISC frameworks programme[1] has been offering a variety of advisory services for integrated information environments, such as MLE development. The technical and tools framework deals with infrastructural issues. For instance, the 'Creating MLEs InfoKit' begins by exploring how to understand an organisation and only then suggests techniques for gathering requirements and designing an MLE.[2]

This book is not recommending a specific method for rethinking university and college processes; each institution will, of course, build on its own experiences. There were, however, four important and generally applicable results from this specific scoping study (even though it was not actually implemented, due to changes in the external context):

1   It showed the importance of first defining project scope.
2   The methodology for mapping what already exists and proposing changes was itself an effective way to get buy-in and validation from key stakeholders.
3   It offered an effective means of concentrating on student focus and taking attention away from functional interests and silos. It therefore enabled staff buy-in by offering the shared aim of improving the student experience.
4   It provided a useful means of highlighting key points within and across processes for adding value – either by reducing duplication or by providing services where there were previously problematic gaps.

Many institutions are already exploiting the possibilities of more integrated processes, whether as one-stop shops for recruitment, enrolment and other student services or through portals, MLEs and regional networks. They are integrating parts of processes where this is perceived as having some benefits and is feasible to implement (although usually without challenging existing functions and departments too radically).

Some have been able to take a more strategic approach to adding value. As well as mapping existing processes, they have critically reviewed the whole or key parts of the organisation (by using the cost–benefit and risks assessments as outlined in Chapter 7 or through equivalent methods) so as to develop clear aims and objectives for an integrated approach. And they are developing an understanding of the potential of Web-based data networks for:

- improving existing processes:
  - by removing gaps and duplications and building in increased responsiveness;
  - by making more effective, creative and multiple use of data;
  - by making more effective, creative and flexible staff and students' activities.
- redesigning existing processes to make them perform better;
- adding new processes where these build on existing specialisms;
- removing or reallocating services where these are inefficient or inappropriate.

How, then, can new developments in ICT offer improved services and added value to universities and colleges?

Exploiting Web-based opportunities for adding value

Let us now return to the properties of Web-enabled business processes that might be relevant to post-compulsory education, as outlined in Chapter 4. Here, we can explore in more detail some of the opportunities for e-business development within each of the quadrants that Fingar *et al.* (1999) defined (see Figure 8.2).

In each of these quadrants – the information/knowledge market, customer relationship management, stakeholder relationship management, supply chain management and educational services – we can apply Lam and Harrison-Walker's (2003) objectives framework (also introduced in Chapter 4) so as to explore what kind of added value e-enabled services can offer. It should be noted that the scope of this exercise has been deliberately

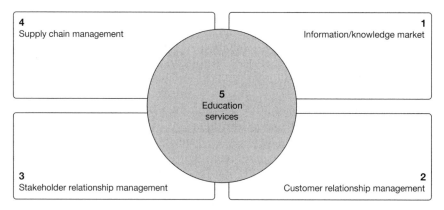

Figure 8.2 Web-enabled business processes for post-compulsory education.
Source: adapted from Fingar *et al.* 1999.

constrained, for simplicity's sake, to only consider Web-enabled services, as opposed to wider technological opportunities such as the application of Radio Frequency Identification (RFID) or other technologies to education services. It is also true that information and communication technologies continue to change so rapidly that all we can offer here are a few suggestions, which may be soon outdated or superseded. The aim is only to indicate the kinds of enhancements that are possible, not to provide a comprehensive list of alternatives.

Quandrant 1: Web-enabled information/knowledge markets

The central activity of any university or college involves the effective communication of knowledge and information, whether from teachers, student support staff and academic administrators to students, from students to students, between staff, or between staff and other stakeholders (both internal and external). There has been a considerable amount of work published on writing organisational information strategies (for example, as part of the JISC Information Strategies Initiative[3]), but our understanding of the impact of Web-enabled technologies on knowledge or information content, its 'containers' and its effective transfer is still relatively poor. Also, as Liz Orna has shown, information management is often treated as a technical issue, separate from how people relate to it (Orna 2005).

Drawing on a subset of the relational and value-based objectives that Lam and Harrison-Walker (2003) identify we can propose a number of aspects offered by the new Web-enabled information and knowledge markets (see Table 8.1).

As an example of a clearly thought-out business strategy to move to Web-enabled implementation, the Massachusetts Institute of Technology (MIT) famously made the decision in 2001 to make all of its course materials publicly accessible online. This was based on a visioning exercise with consultants, resulting in the university explicitly 'bolstering the intellectual commons' (Abelson 2002: 34) through OpenCourseware[4] the Open Knowledge Initiative (creating an open source, open software learning platform for all universities to use) and D-Space (an equivalent to the course materials repository but for research publications). As Abelson says:

> A lot of people point to this being an altruistic gesture on the part of MIT, but in cold business terms I don't view this as an altruistic gesture at all. MIT is much more a consumer of course material than it is a producer of course material: any university is. MIT, at least, is very much about the interaction between faculty and students that happens on campus . . . I view it as a way to preserve university values in the face of the threat of commercialisation of this thing called courseware.
>
> (2002: 34)

Table 8.1 Examples of Web-enabled information/knowledge markets for post-compulsory education

---

Direct access

- Websites provide direct access, without intermediaries, to a university or college's information and resources; and enable potential applicants to engage directly with initial services such as applying on-line
- Many other services could be provided in this context e.g.,
  - Online profiling, enabling the applicant to choose the most appropriate course
  - Online careers advice
  - Course materials 'tasters'
  - Customised marketing to potential customers (email invites to events/news updates)
  - Personalised access for existing students (remembers their previous preferences/suggests alternatives)

Network development

- With online forums and instant messaging (e.g. Facebook and MSN), the next generation of students is already well versed in communicating through networks. University websites can provide forums for different groupings, such as alumni from a particular course, who can then act as mentors for existing students
- Networks also enable existing students and alumni to add information to a university website, developing peer reviews and knowledge repositories. The current debate about Web 2.0 focuses on what Tim O'Reilly calls 'Harnessing Collective Intelligence' (O'Reilly 2005) with 'rich' and collective user experiences, often driven by networked information-sharing. Peer-supported learning processes are a natural extension of this
- Well-designed conferencing systems supported by training in e-moderating can enhance both face-to-face and e-learning methods

Financial improvement

- HE institutions already act as brokers for accommodation services, the provision of which they have increasingly outsourced. To extend this, institutions could also act as intermediaries (for commission) with existing organisations to provide other commercial transactions, such as retail – academic book-selling services, stationery, computer equipment – or insurance services directly from the institution website
- Given the shift to fees in HE, this could even include online auctions to 'sell' different courses at different rates to successful applicants[a]
- The potential of e-learning as a revenue-generating Web-based service is still undeveloped; whether providing free materials as a means of attracting 'customers', offering subscriptions or selling educational products

Product and channel enrichment

- High-quality associated services such as student digital radio/television broadcasts, downloadable lectures to computers or iPods (podcasts), and mobile streaming
- Online tools in support of learning such as blogs/digital storage and display, and intelligent searching for users, including the ability to answer questions/deliver customised responses (see Google Answers and Yahoo's similar recent venture)
- Following Amazon, data tracking and personalisation; student-to-student review etc.
- Develop course materials using innovative new technologies such as gaming/augmented reality/VR, e.g. Linden Lab's Second Life

---

a See earlier discussions and NEA's Market driven futures, www2.nea.org/he/future/market.html

MIT has thus been very innovative in using the development of the Web to enhance their brand identity, while refusing to 'go commercial'. Public availability of these materials attracts students, enhances the university's reputation and does not in any way undermine the staff's intellectual property rights; materials are proven to be only partial without the tutors' involvement – the 'value added' of tuition, beyond the bare materials themselves, becomes evident. More recently, Stanford University has begun offering a range of podcasts of lectures and other educational materials via Apple's iTunes service.

Other educational institutions have also been innovative (see, for example, Glasgow Caledonian University[5] but probably the best – and extremely popular – public service and educational example in the UK is the BBC[6] mainly because it has invested in the specialist expertise – content managers, Web designers, metadata experts and so on – to support its activities.

Quadrant 2: Web-enabled customer relationship management

As outlined in Chapter 3, one of the core elements of an e-business is customer focus. Universities and colleges are increasingly using portals as a way of letting students and staff access information across both academic and administrative functions (for instance, fee and personal details data as well as e-learning). These offer a valuable 'co-ordinated' tool for joining-up previously disparate systems, but do not often *start* from an analysis of what a truly student-focused, Web-enabled support service could be like. Many businesses have developed Customer Relationship Management (CRM) systems, here outlined by the Australian National Office for the Information Economy in their study of e-business practices within the Australian university and college sector:

> Briefly defined, CRM is an integrated sales, marketing and service strategy that depends on co-ordinated enterprise-wide actions, not the actions of individual staff members. CRM software helps organisations manage customer relationships better by tracking customer interactions of all types. The suite of CRM software products available on the market span all the steps of the selling and customer service cycle to help automate direct-mail marketing campaigns, telemarketing, telesales, lead qualification, response management, lead tracking, opportunity management, quotes and order configuration.
>
> (NOIE 2002: 82)

Applications of fully integrated CRM software in an HE and FE context are few and far between, particularly in institutions that are not primarily distance-learning focused. This is also a response to problems with CRM systems which, like many commercial technology products, may not be best suited to an educational context.

In general, what we can observe in the post-compulsory education environment in the UK is a more piecemeal approach (for instance, most MLEs could be seen as merely a partially implemented response to CRM). What is crucial is that customer care is about refocusing the institution towards the integrated set of processes through which students interact with a university or college – from the student's point of view. This is not to advocate CRM as the single solution, but is about using the systems approach inherent within its framework as a means of exploring what an integrated customer service might be like. Kalakota and Robinson suggest that a CRM framework would have three objectives:

1   to use existing relationships to grow revenue (it is cheaper to sell to an existing customer than to find a new customer);
2   to use integrated information to provide excellent service;
3   to provide consistent, replicable sales channel processes and procedures.

(2001: 172–3)

As an example of best practice, the Securities Institute of Australia developed a comprehensive approach to CRM, using a dedicated software platform. This required a joint initiative between the suppliers and the institution: to customise a CRM package to meet their specific needs; to undergo a substantial re-engineering of their existing business processes; and to invest in a technology infrastructure that lent itself to integration (NOIE 2002: 10–4). However, at the end of this structural change, the institution defined the following tangible and intangible benefits:

> The tangible benefits include improved customer relations and services; more efficient work processes; and the availability of valuable information about customers' behaviour and preferences. The Securities Institute case study also suggests that a macro benefit of CRM is the ability for educational organisations to analyse detailed data about customers, which could lead to fundamental review of the way the organisation acquires, supports and retains customers, which in turn could lead to a re-engineering of the organisation.
>
> The intangible benefits of CRM include removing a sense of the educational organisation serving different groups or silos of students, and replacing that approach with a sense that each student is receiving individualised service. Another intangible benefit, apparent from the Securities Institute case study, is that the fragmentation of information

about any one customer across different sections of the organisation can be replaced by the consolidation of information about any one customer, leading to better decisions about serving that customer.

(NOIE 2002: 83–4)

Whatever approaches post-compulsory educational institutions in the UK look to in order to better integrate student support, these are significant benefits. For most institutions, this will mean first analysing the processes that already happen (as discussed above) and developing strategies for integrating different parts of the organisations and different systems. Table 8.2 offers some examples of the kinds of improvement that Web-enabled customer care can offer.

It has been suggested throughout this book that post-compulsory education has a close fit with e-business definitions of customer focus – by its very nature, education is about longer term and typically profoundly engaged interactions with students. This relationship, for many institutions, will commence before a student is enrolled, with student recruitment activities and admissions preceding the point at which the student becomes a 'member' of the institution. There are then the three or four years that a student spends at a university, for example, and a subsequent alumni relationship that is less deep but may be sustained for perhaps decades, at a much lower level of engagement. This understanding of the student as a 'member' of the university or college, with a long-term involvement with (and loyalty to) their institution has already been explored in previous chapters.

This suggests that post-compulsory education possesses a characteristic that, ironically perhaps, many e-businesses seek to emulate in implementing CRM. Students, whether we view them as customers or not, perceive themselves as part of the educational community (in the sense of Rappa's e-business model noted in Chapter 4). Membership, as a concept, transcends being a 'customer': it implies identification and involvement with the institution beyond the simple financial transaction. It implies some level of ownership and of belonging. This is the relationship that many e-businesses are seeking to develop in their own customer base through the level of engagement and personalisation afforded by effective CRM. Amazon, which has been mentioned several times before, is a good example of a business pursuing the membership concept: the range of activities and services Amazon offers its customers through its site encourages engagement beyond the 'buy'. Amazon's reliance upon its users to provide reviews and ratings of the products it sells has produced both a competitive advantage for Amazon, in terms of the value placed upon reviews by customers, and a higher level of engagement among some customer-users, conferring a membership status upon them – they have some measure of ownership of the site's content. The underpinning technology and Amazon's 'vision' of business

Table 8.2 Examples of Web-enabled customer care for post-compulsory education

---

Direct access

- Reduce costs by increasing self-service aspects, particularly in terms of students controlling their own data
- Extend the range of student direct access services to include customer care aspects; for example, in supporting teaching and learning materials, in self-assessing learning skills and styles, in online booking and in conferencing with student support staff online
- Aim for Unique Learner Number (ULN) – offering a single point of authentication (see Signposter, Box 1.1, Chapter 1)
- Enable potential applicants to apply directly and to undergo online aptitude testing/be assessed for a place on a course (for example, through the uniTEST process[a])

Network development

- Integrate personnel and other data across the network, so that inputs and updating are consistent, robust and secure, enabling the student to have a 'one-stop' service from any part of the system
- Track data effectively across different areas and enable appropriate real-time access
- Use intelligent searching and monitoring of data across networks to offer 'early warning' of student academic and pastoral difficulties

Financial improvement

- Institutions can significantly reduce the costs associated with processing applications and other associated administrative and financial transactions
- Integrate student entry with student lifecycle transactions to prevent duplication and gaps and to improve retention through an integrated yet confidential response to student problems
- Institutions can increase revenue – for example, via a campus debit card, which enables students to make payments for food on campus and at the bookshop and other stores, using an account set up and maintained by the institution

Product and channel enrichment

- Personalised portals as a single point of access to all university services can offer students a unified experience across educational, personal and social needs
- The provision of a range of online support materials and services, which students can self select to support their own development; and choose a preferred medium (e.g. audio, video, graphics, text)

---

a See www.unitest.org.uk/

process (especially the recommendations aspect) delivers an integrated and customer-oriented environment that seeks to sustain longer term, personalised relationships with customers. Jeff Bezos, Amazon's CEO, in a guest lecture at MIT, highlighted one consequence of their intimate and individualised knowledge of customer buying: Amazon introduced a 'duplicates warning' feature for CDs, so that customers wouldn't buy the same CD twice. The level of CD sales dropped somewhat as a result, but levels of customer satisfaction (and therefore the likelihood of maintaining longer term, satisfying relationships) increased (Bezos 2002).

When CRM is done well, it produces substantial benefits for the providing organisation, but it should also deliver perceived benefits to customers/ members. Post-compulsory education has some inherent affinity with the nature of the CRM process, but institutions generally have yet to make the most of such opportunities.

Quadrant 3: Web-enabled stakeholder management

Educational institutions have a wide range of formal external stakeholders, as complex as that of many large businesses, particularly in terms of relationships with employer organisations, financing bodies and government agencies. All of these require different kinds of analysis, reporting and regulatory frameworks. Historically, post-compulsory education has dealt with these stakeholders separately, sometimes to the extent of often not knowing precisely the number and range of relationships held across an institution at any one time.

Meanwhile, quality management has become an increasingly high profile and essential component of provision. Ernst *et al.* (1994) argue that public expectations and government involvement will lead to more reporting requirements and accountability. Although they are talking about the American experience, there are many overlaps with the UK:

> The ultimate effect of the concurrent rise [in] tuition and decrease in the availability of college-eligible students will be an increase in public scrutiny of colleges and universities. In what some characterise as an emerging buyer's market for higher education, parents, students, donors, research sponsors and legislators will demand increasing institutional accountability for the quality of all aspects of campus activity.
>
> Such pressures demand a corresponding re-think of our operations ... [T]he increased need for public accountability trumpet(s) the limitations of bureaucracy as higher education's prevailing control strategy. In effect, our strategy to date has had to allow the prevention of transaction errors to shape and define our administrative structures and systems. In creating a never-ending cycle of audits, proceduralisation,

forms generation, signature authorisation and centralisation of decision-making, we have lost sight of our constituents and have created administration for its own sake and a culture averse to risk.'

(Ernst *et al.*, 1994: 10)

As illustrated in Figure 1.1 (Chapter 1), Ernst, Katz and Sack argue instead for less rule-governed and more streamlined operations that depend on employee judgements and greater delegation of authority. This is because information technologies and architectures focus on customised and secure access to data and workflow processes, rather than old-fashioned paper trails and paper-based signature as the monitoring and control mechanism. They therefore outline a related series of old and new strategies for stakeholder management, around the twin Web-enabled capabilities of self-service access and enhanced data control and reporting. From this view, information (although it must remain robust and secure) is not so much for capturing and storing as for distributing and exchanging. Table 8.3 gives examples of strategies driven by this approach.

These strategies also have relevance for the 'internal' stakeholders – the university or college staff. For instance, part of Cisco's redesign of their working practices has been to put more control over data in the hands of staff, such as by self-reporting on travel and other expenses. Instead of a bureaucratic process of signatures and circulating paperwork, staff claim online. This is seen as the negotiation of acceptable risk; payments are monitored and randomly checked by a small team for accuracy and appropriateness. Some other examples of Web-enabled improvements to stakeholder management are given in Table 8.4.

Quadrant 4: Web-enabled supply chain management

Emerging technologies are enabling an increased ease of data transfer and analysis, coupled with online tracking, customised reporting, events notification and robust security and authentication. All of these can enhance supply-chain processes. There are many examples of e-procurement in use, especially in low-value, high-quantity areas such as library acquisition, computers and stationery. The Australian National Office of the Information Economy examined e-procurement in relation to Australian universities and colleges:

Traditional methods of purchasing supplies involved the preparation of a paper-based order, manual authorisation of the order and the manual dispatch of the purchase order. E-Procurement involves the ordering of goods electronically, ideally using a Web-based platform, involving suppliers' online catalogues and buyers ordering online. E-Payment

Table 8.3 Strategies for relating to stakeholders

Old strategy	New strategy
Introduce new rules	Specify desired outcomes
Introduce new forms	Negotiate acceptable risk
Acquire additional signatures	Embed controls in ICT
Centralise approval authority	Measure and evaluate continuously
Write new reports	Integrated data exchange from sink to source
Information politics: feudalism	Information politics: federalism
Transaction applications have integrated reporting	Reporting is separate to transaction capture
Need to tell: desk-top publishing	Need to know: knowledge repositories

Source: adapted from Ernst *et al.* 1994.

Table 8.4 Examples of Web-enabled stakeholder management

Direct access

* Reduce costs by increasing self-service aspects, particularly in control of own data
* Take data consumers' task perspective rather than data owners' functional perspective
* Open up data to stakeholders as producers as well as consumers, rather than restrict to administrative staff; enable sharing whilst maintaining security and robustness of information

Network development

* Integrated data exchange throughout organisation, and between organisation and partners
* Continuing Professional Development (CPD) through online learning packages, supported by peer-reviewed knowledge repositories, enabling the sharing of up-to-date organisation and subject-related materials
* Digital research repositories link organisations, so as to share cutting-edge developments quickly and effectively (see Text Box in Chapter 5)

Financial improvement

* Saves costs through self-service access and effective reporting
* Extends range of services institution can either out-source or effectively provide beyond its own boundaries; such as providing accreditation and QA services, exploiting IPR, selling or sharing educational content and selling, brokering or sharing other services and facilities

systems can enhance an e-Procurement system. Electronic ordering sometimes enables purchasers to avoid some of the 'middlemen' stages of the supply chain, so that the buyer avoids retailers, marketers and distributors, placing the order directly with the manufacturer – a phenomenon called 'disintermediation'.

(NOIE 2002: 80)

For effective Web-enabled relationships with suppliers, commonly agreed standards become essential. In Australia, the Australian Procurement and Construction Council (APCC) developed a Government Framework for National Cooperation on Electronic Procurement in 2000, based on the benefits for government, industry and education of a co-ordinated framework for the implementation of e-Procurement.

In the UK, the London Universities Purchasing Consortium (LUPC)[7] operates as an independent organisation orchestrating supplier services to London-based government organisations by bringing institutions and suppliers together within a common framework (see Figure 8.3). The value of consortia such as these is not only to reduce costs but also to improve the procurement process as a whole (and give institutions, as buyers, more leverage in the marketplace). There are other UK consortia such as Crescent Purchasing Consortium specifically set up for FE colleges. Some organisations, however, find that direct interaction with a supplier can produce other benefits, particularly in enabling close relationships to be formed.

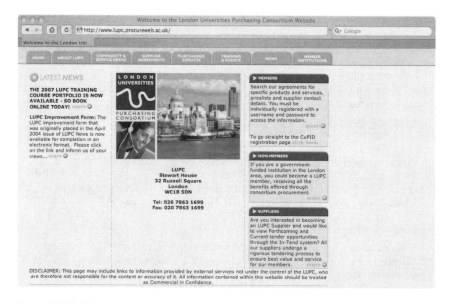

Figure 8.3 LUPC e-procurement website.

As well as e-procurement, an e-business approach, in the context of integrated, virtual value chains, can lead to redesigned relationships with suppliers in terms of access to data. This is sometimes described as out-tasking rather than outsourcing. Here, secure channels enable data to be shared beyond the institution, although control remains within it. The IBM e-business model, known as 'on-demand' (which will be explored in greater detail in Chapter 9), argues that a really transformational e-business approach requires the out-tasking or outsourcing of as many non-core activities as possible. This is seen as having two benefits. First, the educational institution can be very flexible in its response to changing contexts since it has reduced its fixed costs. Second, other organisations then provide specialised services to the whole post-secondary educational sector, which both minimises their own risk and enables the development of improved expertise. Table 8.5 illustrates some other example areas of Web-enabled supply chain management.

There are now a large number of suppliers to education, particularly in relation to e-learning. These offer a wide range of services: technological platforms, delivery services (for example, Personal Development Plans or assessment), course and curriculum development, content repositories, distribution, accommodation and specialist facilities, education consultancies, administrative and business services, intellectual property management, publishing and marketing (Matkin 2002: 5–12). Post-compulsory educational institutions are, therefore, increasingly having to decide between procuring such services externally and providing them in-house.

Table 8.5 Examples of Web-enabled supply chain management

Direct access

Have direct, online access between suppliers and purchasers with shared data and real-time updating

Network development

Integrate data across the network, for enhanced workflow/process management

Financial improvement

Can significantly reduce the costs associated with procurement and supply-chain management and other associated administrative and financial transactions

Product and channel enrichment

Enables closer links with preferred suppliers and increased leverage (buyer power) in the marketplace.

Sector 5: Web-enabled education services

At the centre of Figure 8.2 lies education services, one of the three core activities previously identified. As noted above, e-learning developments are often more visible in the Web-enabled spectrum of education, as it forms a primary-level activity (in value-chain terms), compared to the secondary or support activities. As was discussed in Chapter 4, Matkin's typology of educational strategies and services offers a number of discrete applications of technology, beyond traditional learning, ranging from blended learning through to distance learning (Matkin 2002). However, although there are many fine examples of online educational materials, most universities and colleges are not yet exploiting the full potential of existing Web capabilities, let alone grappling with the implications for teaching and learning of the endless stream of new and increasingly sophisticated software and networking applications. As noted in Chapter 5, there remain many barriers to the 'roll-out' of electronic course materials and delivery mechanisms, including risk, staff resistance and cost frameworks.

The NMC–NLII (2005: 4) *Horizon Report*, which brings together Silicon Valley technology professionals with US college and university representatives, lists six trends 'likely to have a large impact on teaching, learning or creative expression within higher education'. In the immediate future they predict that both wireless technologies and extended learning – the integration of classroom teaching with online instruction and the support of various communication tools – will become ubiquitous. The *Horizon Report* authors see education shifting to incorporate mobile devices in the classroom, as well as improving integration between online and face-to-face provision by concentrating support materials electronically, allowing class time for more personal and diagnostic interaction (NMC–NLII 2005: 11–13). In addition, they suggest that the following four areas will become much more prevalent over the years to 2010:

1   *Intelligent Searching*: there is increasing availability of tools that enable students to precisely locate, retrieve and organise information from a wide variety of sources (own and networked computers, intranet and Internet, mobile devices, etc.). This is both through customised and personalised search agents and via specialist search engines. Content can also be made accessible in a wide variety of formats and through an increasing number of devices (NMC–NLII 2005: 14–16).

2   *Educational Gaming*: a considerable amount of development is taking place both in examining how existing gaming environments might be adapted to education and in how 'learning through play' offers some productive techniques for teaching. Gaming often exploits the possibilities of virtual reality and immersive environments, but is not solely reliant on them (NMC–NLII 2005: 17–19).

3 *Social Networks and Knowledge Webs*: the rise of interactive communications such as texting, instant messaging (IM), together with blogs and social networking services such as Flickr and del.icio.us (supported by very simple-to-use technologies) has been very evident over the past few years. This growth (and the current wave of interest in Web 2.0) suggests the increased significance of social networking and interpersonal connections (rather than the diminution of social contact that was once seen as a consequence of ICT). These offer forms of peer collaboration and communication that can powerfully supplement conventional tutor–student relationships. The authors argue that '*Learners are not only willing to participate in the construction of knowledge; they are starting to expect to*' (NMC–NLII 2005: 2).

4 *Context-Aware Computing/Augmented Reality*: context-aware computing uses environmental conditions to customise the user's experience or options. Augmented reality provides additional contextual information that appears as part of the user's world (NMC–NLII 2005: 23–5).

All of these illustrate how the speed and connectivity of new technologies and networks are being quickly incorporated into everyday life. Future educational application must take into account such technological change.

Towards transformation?

It has been suggested throughout this book that most universities and colleges are automating and integrating some of their processes but not moving too far from traditional educational practices and processes. Even work on MLEs tends to start from the learning and teaching sphere, such as an existing VLE or the management information systems (MIS) and then 'adds on' other services, rather than starting from a completely integrated model. An integrated approach is one that, from the student's point of view, describes integrated processes (student entry, managing the student experience, facilitating learning and curriculum development, etc.) which bridge across, and do not differentiate between, academic, administrative and student support provision.

How, then, might a university or college move towards transformation of some or all of its core business processes? Although it could be argued that we think we know what we are doing in post-compulsory education and that it will be too expensive/time-consuming/risk-producing to revisit, this chapter has shown that it remains very important to:

• map what already exists;
• go beyond a focus on targets and look at change in support of improved outcomes;

- shift the whole approach from being orientated towards teachers or administrative staff to being personalised to individual applicants/students/alumni ('members');
- develop an understanding of how new Web-based technologies open up new areas for improved services.

The next, and final, chapter of this book, returns to the MIT 90s model to consider just how a post-compulsory institution might move from the lower levels to a more transformational approach to ICT and educational services.

Notes

1   See JISC website www.jisc.ac.uk/index.cfm?name=programme_frameworks.
2   See JISC website www.jiscinfonet.ac.uk/InfoKits/creating-an-mle.
3   See JISC website www.jisc.org.uk/index.cfm?name=programme_infstrat.
4   The materials are available at http://ocw.mit.edu.
5   See Glasgow Caledonian University website www.gcal.ac.uk/shopping.
6   See BBC website www.bbc.co.uk.
7   See London Universities Purchasing Consortium website www.lupc.procureweb. ac.uk.

Bibliography

Abelson, H. (2002) 'MIT, the Internet, and the commons of the mind', in *Teaching as E-business? Research and Policy Agendas*. Selected Conference Proceedings, Center for Studies in Higher Education (CSHE), University of California, Berkeley, October 2001: pp. 31–40.

Bezos, J. (2002) 'Earth's most customer centric company: differentiating with technology'. MIT School of Engineering guest lecture. Online. Available at http://mitworld.mit.edu/video/1/ (accessed 15 December 2005).

Ernst, D.J., Katz, R.N. and Sack, J.R. (1994) *Organisational and Technological Strategies for Higher Education in the Information Age*. CAUSE Professional Papers Series, No.13.

Fingar, P., Kumar, H. and Sharma, T. (1999) '21st century markets: from places to spaces', *First Monday*, 4 (12) December. Online. Available at www.firstmonday.dk/issues/issue4_12/fingar/index.html (accessed 15 December 2005).

Hammer, M. (1990) 'Reengineering work: don't automate, obliterate', *Harvard Business Review* July–August: 104–112.

JISC (2005) 'Infonet Managed Learning Environment (MLE) toolkit'. Online. Available at www.jiscinfonet.ac.uk/InfoKits/creating-an-mle/understanding-your-organisation/finding-out-what-really-happens (accessed 1 August 2005)

Kalakota, R. and Robinson, M. (2001) *E-Business 2.0: strategies for success*. Reading, MA: Addison-Wesley.

Lam, Long W. and Harrison-Walker, L. Jean (2003) 'Towards an objective-based typology of e-business models', *Business Horizons* November–December: 17–26.

Matkin, G. (2002) 'Developing a conceptual framework and vocabulary for e-learning', in *Teaching as E-business? Research and Policy Agendas*. Selected Conference Proceedings, Center for Studies in Higher Education (CSHE), University of California, Berkeley, October 2001.

NMC–NLII (2005) 'Horizon report', New Media Consortium–National Learning Infrastructure Initiative Online. Available at www.nmc.org/pdf/2005_Horizon_Report.pdf (accessed 15 December 2005).

NOIE (2002) 'e-Business in education', DCITA, June. Online. Available at www.dcita.gov.au/ie/publications/2002/june/ebusiness_in_education (accessed 15 December 2005).

Orna, L. (2005) *Making Knowledge Visible*. Aldershot, UK and Burlington, VT: Gower.

Osterwalder, A. and Pigneur, Y. (2002) 'An e-business model ontology for modeling e-business', 15th Bled Electronic Commerce Conference – e-Reality: Constructing the e-Economy (Bled, Slovenia), 17–19 June.

Chapter 9

Getting from here to there

From evolution to transformation

Graham Hill

Implementing e-business systems in large and complex organisations is notoriously difficult and risk prone, but, as this book has suggested these systems can transform business efficiency and levels of customer service. Successful implementation requires resources, technical expertise, project management, organisational re-engineering and change-management to be fused into a harmonious whole. There are many examples of very successful projects that not only delivered on time, but also exceeded customer expectations. However, this is not always achieved and, unfortunately, system implementation failures are also common. Given the difficult and far-reaching nature of implementation projects, there is great potential for misconceptions, misunderstandings, errors of judgement and oversights that can cause serious problems and induce projects to fail. Small systems, those with only a handful of users, largely self-contained and subject to very few external pressures, are often developed, installed and operated with few problems. Large systems, those that are complex, span multiple business functions, cross numerous organisational boundaries (both within and outside the institution) and embrace different technologies provide a greater challenge. Their selection and implementation projects are often long, usually spanning several years from first conception and investigation through to the final conclusion.

Most post-compulsory educational institutions are already creating joined-up learning and administrative environments – managed learning environments (MLEs). Here, the difficulties and risks of implementing large, complex systems can consume vast amounts of time, drain budgets and exhaust the personnel involved. The difficulties are considerable, requiring agile decision-making, creation and extension of alliances and partnerships, establishment of new performance metrics, and all of this at an accelerating pace. But HE and FE institutions know that, at some level, they need to respond constructively to the pace and risk of technological change. Senior managers are increasingly putting e-business on the organisational agenda and there is a recognised need for e-business initiatives. This is because the Internet, and the increasing connectivity associated with it, has introduced a new environment, which represents both a threat and an opportunity to current activities within post-compulsory education. The potential exists to lower costs, create new markets, sustain new services, and positively support customers and stakeholders enabling a transformation of the student experience. And, as shown in Chapter 5, the Web also provides the environment for intense national and international competition, and the capability for new entrants to operate effectively across the educational marketplace.

Although many ICT developments by universities and colleges have been piecemeal and unco-ordinated, this book has described the landscape for educational organisations to move towards revolutionary e-business activity. Some UK institutions, including the universities of Warwick, Strathclyde and Bradford[1] (see Box 9.1), have formally recognised e-business initiatives. US exemplars include Buena Vista (Thinkpad University)[2], Case Western Reserve (leading on portal developments)[3] and North Carolina (award-winning best practice)[4].

So how can universities and colleges deliver successful projects at a larger and more integrated scale? This chapter draws together a number of specific areas for consideration within the HE and FE sectors, examining some of the lessons learned, highlighting best practice and considering the implications. It will follow the same methodology as the previous chapters by using the MIT 90s model to explore different levels of change, from evolutionary, through transitional and onto transformational. As before, the preliminary stage of localised and co-ordinated use (evolutionary) is defined as the automation of current processes; the transitional stage as encompassing higher levels of integration, focused on embedding the use of ICT and developing innovative uses; with the transformational or revolutionary stage involving the development of new processes that do things differently.

Organisational considerations

This book has explored e-business as a means of learning lessons for HE and FE. It does not advocate a particular model or a specific approach. In considering implementation, five general points – adapted from Booz-Allen Hamilton Inc. (2006) – can be stated initially:

1 One size does not fit all

Each organisation must develop and drive its own e-business strategy, based on an analysis of the broader external environment in which it operates. It will require the organisation and its resources to be mobilised to maximise the likelihood of success (see Chapter 6). Key factors will not be the same for different types of organisation and a clear understanding of where the institution is now is an essential prerequisite.

Box 9.1 Case Study: University of Bradford

At Bradford University three elements of e-strategy were embedded within the corporate plan 2004-2009. These were:

- A Web-enabled campus supported by mobile computing and wireless networking
- Smart administration for flexible learners
- A teaching and learning strategy that integrates key skills, one of which is 'communicating in an information age'

The e-strategy projects will ultimately deliver more than the 'sum of their individual parts' – some are infrastructure, some are content, all are ultimately student-focused. On its own, each project may not alter the overall student experience, but taken together as a coherent package they may enable the university to differentiate its offering. Incremental capital funding of £11 million over 5 years was initially identified to be delivered in two tranches. A new PVC portfolio (Strategic Systems Development) was introduced in 2004 to focus the university's e-strategy. An e-strategy board was established reporting to the Vice-Chancellors Group, which comprised academic, e-learning, research, IT, finance and planning expertise, but resources were not explicitly dedicated to e-business activity. The e-strategy board are required to provide monthly tracking reports to inform the university's Balanced Scorecard, which is reporting compliance and delivery against the Corporate Plan.

2 Managing a programme

Different institutions are already pursuing simultaneously a number of projects that could properly be described as enabling aspects of e-business. However, they may not be coherent in approach and are likely to be meeting various operational needs, with different funding and resource structures and requiring a diverse range of skills. The key need is for a focused and managed approach. Implementing an e-business strategy should deliver a programme that is greater than the sum of its constituent parts.

3 E-business opportunities are not the same

Elsewhere we have described the range of initiatives from evolutionary through revolutionary – that is, from extending existing information and services and delivering online, to creating entirely new business opportunities. Each opportunity needs to be developed appropriately to its context, which will effect how implementation is carried out.

4 There are some common approaches

Research with corporate CEOs and top e-business executives around the world suggests a consistent path that companies have already followed to get 'from here to there'. The Cisco approach (see Chapter 3) is one such, but the sector also needs to be accumulating good practice examples specifically relevant to education. Learning from these implementation projects can help post-secondary education meet the challenges more effectively and improve its chances of success.

5 People are key

Attracting and retaining the right talent is crucial to success and needs to include the necessary incentives to enable us to compete successfully. Many educators already have a significant understanding of Internet technologies and our student customers represent a 'captive' and 'engaged' community, which enables us to experiment and develop transformational ideas. Finding the right blend of skills including technical, project management and business/academic knowledge is the central issue, not merely the technology itself.

Stage 1: e-business evolution through information automation and co-ordination

This stage is characterised by the use of Internet technologies to provide access to information and to improve both internal and external communication. Post-compulsory educational institutions have been in the vanguard of developments as the pioneers and early adopters of Web technologies. Web-based systems from email to intranet to e-learning to e-procurement are now integral to post-compulsory education. Advances in email technology on the desk and through Web interfaces have transformed our ability to communicate anytime, anywhere through simple interchangeable tools whether at our desk, at home, on the move on laptops and phones. We provide comprehensive levels of static information to our campus communities (intranet) and to our potential customers and partners (extranet). Our organisations have always adopted transparent access to information, but in recent years we have been able to exploit technology to provide well-structured information on a significant scale, increasingly using sophisticated means of searching and presenting information in corporate styles. We have seen exponential increases in the amount of information available in this way, and also in the volume of 'self service' requests to download and view, potentially saving administrative costs.

However, this stage of e-business development is characterised by different initiatives underway throughout the organisation. Often these are local to a particular department or business process but increasingly co-ordinated in some way. The impact of the Internet on the organisation may have registered on the senior management agenda but is not yet a corporate priority. Resources may have been allocated within organisational units but represent a range of seemingly disjointed activities. Perhaps the Internet is still perceived as a series of websites providing information and occasional interactive services. Most of us will recognise this stage and as awareness grows, we appreciate the potential and exploit specific opportunities. However, the lessons that are learned through the various projects are not necessarily shared, and it is likely that the organisation is spending more than it believes on e-business initiatives across the campus (because the staff opportunity cost of such endeavours is often ignored). Without central co-ordination or strategic direction the activities may appear, and probably are, confusing and inefficient. There are many institutions with dozens, even hundreds of websites and Web servers, which have been developed by various academic and administrative functions, that have no coherence and do not reflect brand image or corporate style, never mind consistency of business process or student experience. This can hold true even where attempts are made to 'contain' disparate information within a Content Management System (CMS). The resources in this phase are inevitably spread thin or projects are not formally resourced at all, and while this phase is a necessary first step in order to develop initial skills and capabilities, organisations may already have begun to move onto a more structured approach. The increasing overall incoherence (and inability to progress 'from the bottom' to a more integrated approach from these piecemeal responses) often acts as a 'push' towards an institutional strategy. The areas initially where this is usually felt most strongly are around consistency and integration of student data (for management information purposes), e-learning services and in reporting to external stakeholders.

The business of education depends on high-quality information transfer – admissions, enrolment, timetabling, assessments, etc. Yet these are still routinely non-integrated, complicated and inaccurate from the students' point of view. Universities and colleges have already invested significant amounts in transforming organisational information into digital assets in order to be more efficient and effective. Often these projects have focused on administrative efficiency improvements and more integrated information flows – moving towards the goal of entering data only once into systems and using it many times for different purposes. At the same time, the annual review of financial, student and other business measures has helped to focus investment in the business systems and improve accuracy of the results through publication of national data-sets and league tables. It also delivers information of significant value in the way we establish our organisational objectives and measure their achievement. Where these 'pushes' towards integration are being dealt with explicitly, strategically and creatively, then the organisation has moved on to the transitional stage.

Stage 2: the transition to e-business integration

The transitional stage describes the period in which a thorough rethink of activity is undertaken. Change agents – those who have power to bring about change across the organisation – begin to reshape activities and focus on key business activities and processes. Opportunities are explored for extracting additional value from the existing business, perhaps through improved efficiency (e.g. online student registration) or through extension of existing provision (e.g. offering some course elements online with innovative aspects such as streaming media or interactive blogs), enabling more cost-effective distribution (e.g. greater volume could be delivered through an online environment unconstrained by physical limitations) or improved student communication (e.g. online applicant process tracking). These opportunities tend to be easier to manage and govern and can improve revenue and potentially reduce costs. Drawing on internal resources and capability and using existing organisational structures to deliver specific projects is the most likely approach in post-compulsory education.

In this phase we begin to move towards dynamic business transactions both inside the institution (with our students and staff) and outside the institution (with suppliers, research and industrial partners). Some institutions have used the term 'Web-enabled campus' to describe the vision of services, support, teaching and research in such a Web-enabled environment. MLE developments mainly fit in this category. There are also a number who have made considerable progress with delivering either stand-alone business transactions, such as student online enrolment or accommodation fee payments, or developed more personalised and customised approaches, which integrate processes together using portal technologies. Many institutions have been early adopters of Web-enabled and database-driven technologies and have fuelled research and development activity on behalf of the whole academic community. Post-compulsory education is uniquely placed to exploit high-speed networking capabilities because it has a well-defined customer base that transacts with academics, student support and administrators each day through teaching, learning and research activity.

It is at this stage however, that we acknowledge the need to organise and form an overall e-business strategy. This will involve the creation of a group with appropriate leadership (see Chapter 6). As said before, an e-business approach is not about the technology chosen for learning, research or administrative systems. There is no shortage of companies and vendors that can deliver solutions to meet the needs of post-compulsory educational institutions. As shown in the previous chapter, universities and colleges must first understand what they already do with data; and how they want to improve its flows and value. This is first and foremost about the quality of the information being held, the appropriateness and effectiveness of its transfer, the way that it is delivered, the ease and control of access and the multiple uses to which it can be put.

So, for example, a significant by-product of better and more integrated systems is the delivery of management information. Many institutions have already created distributed electronic information whether in spreadsheets, databases or some other format that meets specific parochial needs. Tools have been around for some time that enable the information to be used in new and creative ways and allow us to collect and consolidate it effectively. Another example is purchasing of equipment and services. It is not enough to automate the paper order book and introduce a slick operational system to manage procurement electronically. The real significance comes in the management information unlocked, for example:

* who the organisation's top ten suppliers are by value (to enable better negotiation on business value);
* patterns of stationery and IT purchases sourcing (to consolidate purchases and reduce costs);
* amounts spent with a particular supplier last year (to improve negotiations when the contract comes up for renewal).

In Chapter 5, this book explored the need for 'Type 42' management as recommended by Dearing. These managers will increasingly demand and expect high-quality information in order to do their jobs. Delivering this information will enable managers to focus on the appropriate areas to invest effort. In the transitional phase, organisations focus on widespread and transparent access to information, which can open up the use of that information in previously unavailable ways. Some commercial organisations have formed new businesses on the basis of improved understanding and awareness of the information they collected for operational purposes. One example is an insurance company that used its customer database to investigate and drill-down to develop a better understanding of market segments. It found that certain types of customer (female over 40s in certain parts of the country) represented a much lower relative risk and so began to offer lower rates to this group so as to expand its market share. In our business, how much effort do we put into collecting data on different market segments and using this information to exploit possible niches?

Almost all institutions have invested in automated student enquiry and applicant systems to improve the handling and turnaround of enquiries and applicant paperwork. This has improved the operational effectiveness by reducing administrative overheads and integrating some processes. The benefit of adopting database systems to manage this activity is that we can also deliver management information using whatever applicant data we have collected or can derive, and we can also map this against previous years to understand trends and pro-actively manage student intake. As the information quality improves over time we can be much smarter and more sophisticated in our analysis and make better decisions for our organisation.

However, this only works when all areas involved in the process use the same system (codes, rules, process) therefore mandating use of common systems. We can anticipate further significant developments as this stage provides the potential for improved customer service through personalisation and convenience, as well as improved efficiency for our administrative operations. The challenge to implementation of a transitional model is significant. It demands the integration and/or replacement of existing internal systems and business processes in consistent ways across our campuses, that is, a move away from information islands to integrated management information systems. Let us consider a couple of examples that may demonstrate the concept and then consider how this might apply to the education business.

At the low-value end of the spectrum is volume business such as EasyJet. The approach that EasyJet has adopted is to provide a fully integrated no-frills service where transactions are made online direct with the company. The initial service was low-cost flights, which were booked online and managed with paperless, ticketless transactions. The services even included ways for its customers to find the cheapest flights for any particular destination. EasyJet attempts to save its customers money provided they are flexible about travel. Where this company has now exploited this advantage is in extending and integrating its services. Through the same online system you can not only book your flights, but also the coach pickup to the airport, the flight transfers at your destination, car rentals and your check-in to the Easy hotel chain. Even here, the paperless transactions continue with no room keys (you are given a code which expires at the end of your reservation) and no checkout because additional services provided in other hotels, such as mini-bars and guest telephones, are not provided. If you were a student customer, how attractive might it be to transact your business in ways that save you money and that provide a whole range of services in efficient and intelligent ways? And let us consider how many of our students are already EasyJet customers and therefore have this sort of expectation today. As outlined in Chapter 5, what has been called a 'low-end' disruption to existing business practices, based on standardising services and implementing relative pricing for quality of service, is enabling some private sector companies to offer basic but robust educational services.

At the high-value end of the spectrum is niche business, such as pharmaceutical research. One such company called Destiny Pharma developed the world's first light-activated cure for the 'super-bug' MRSA. How did this relatively tiny company manage this innovation to market – effectively punching way above its weight? Although the company has a small core staff it partners with scientists and doctors throughout the world, using technology to conduct its business electronically. It identifies expertise using specialist information directories and forms partnerships through shared commercial incentives. Communication is almost entirely electronic and as an organisation it works on projects around the clock through different time zones. In this way it can be highly flexible and responsive, not just to market forces but also to developing innovative research projects most effectively.

Here, out of coherent data integration and open (but controlled) access, comes new, creative and appropriate uses of information. This, in turn, offers opportunities for a more transformational approach to the educational organisation and its services – to ways of doing things differently.

Stage 3: the on-demand revolution?

In this phase, organisations become responsive to dynamic and unpredictable changes in supply and demand in an effective way. They move costs from fixed to variable so that transaction volumes are not limited by infrastructure and fixed costs are minimised wherever possible. These organisations focus on core competencies and let strategic partners manage selected non-core tasks (at high quality but low transaction cost). Educational institutions have not yet reached this stage for their business and administrative operations, although attempts to implement common systems have been tried in the past. Within the UK National Health Service, and as a result of significant levels of new investment, the concept of shared services between Health Trusts is taking shape as ICT systems are consolidated regionally while business transactions are available on demand at the point of need – potentially patient-led through self-service capability. The ongoing developmental difficulties with computerising and sharing of NHS patient records illustrates just how complex such a shift in organisational patterns and roles is.

Stage 3 on the MIT 90s model is where e-business activities move to the centre of core processes. It brings totally new kinds of transformation through new levels of integration with processes and applications both inside the institution and with the external partners with which it deals. In some cases this may be seeking business services from specialist companies rather than carrying out the activity themselves. The business operations however, are not simply off-loaded (or outsourced) to another company but tightly integrated with invisible joins afforded by technology.

The IBM definition (from which the term comes) of an on-demand business is as follows:

> where business processes – integrated end-to-end across the company and with key partners, suppliers and customers – can respond with

flexibility and speed to customer demand, market opportunity or external threat.

(Palmisano 2003)

The issues here are also about complete and seamless integration, both with customers and with suppliers (Figure 9.1). An example of this phenomenon is the relationship that eBay has established with partners. When you order from eBay you can track the progress of your package delivery using UPS Web services. Although UPS is not owned by eBay it has integrated with this supplier, so it appears as one virtual supply-chain process. You, as the consumer, do not see two companies – only one. A related issue is speed, responsiveness and flexibility. The ultimate aim for an on-demand business is flexibility to alter existing processes to better meet a changing context, by adapting existing ICT systems to new requirements, rather than having to purchase a new generation of bespoke systems.

How, then, does this translate into a wide variety of educational contexts? Les Watson, in Chapter 6, proposed a set of statements defining the innovative or transformational end of the MIT 90s model (Table 9.1).

In a commercial business context this means increasing flexibility and responsiveness to the market by transforming fixed costs into variable costs.

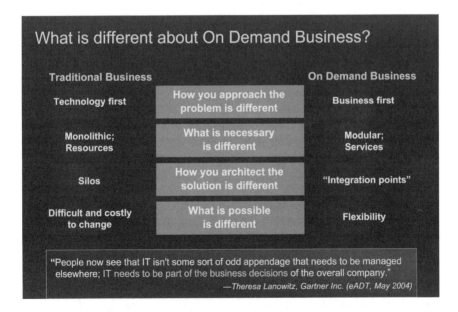

Figure 9.1 What is different about On Demand Business?

Source: from IBM's *On Demand Transformation: creating a great company* (IBM Corporation 2005).

Table 9.1 Transformative levels of action based on MIT 90s model

ICT usage in post-compulsory education	Systems are integrated and distributed access is the norm, including access by external stakeholders
Learning technologies	Institution-wide systems for learner tracking, assessment and learner development used to support all staff and students in their learning
Business processes	Access based on information and service needs to a menu of (Web) services. Emphasis on customised service, together with focus on external reporting, internal monitoring, and forecasting and improvement
Student focus	Student experience environment extends to integration of business and learning systems and provides access to information and transactions with staff trained to deliver in-depth specialist support
Strategy and policy	ICT components of business strategy stimulate new business relationships and models

Source: from Les Watson, Chapter 6.

This might be by out-tasking or outsourcing non-core activities, by collaborating with others so as to share services, or by leveraging more out of existing activities. The organisation is then able to scale-up, scale-down, adapt or transform its core services quickly dependent on demand. But what does this mean in an educational context and what options are available to release the creativity and agility needed to deliver in these new ways? On the demand side for example, as our students require more flexibility in terms of course start dates or course delivery hours (e.g. outside normal teaching hours) or in terms of course content, or we are overwhelmed (or conversely under-whelmed) with well-qualified applicants for a particular course of study, how easy would it be to satisfy that requirement 'on demand'? As we move towards the model of students as customers and/or members, and as they invest significant amounts in their education, we can anticipate a greater demand for this kind of flexibility. As the promotional material states for one such initiative (the collaboration between ICS home learning and University of East London) 'with no set term times you can start when you like, and learn in a completely flexible way, without lectures or seminars to attend' (*The Guardian* 14 February 2006).

On the supply side we employ both fixed and variable assets to perform our existing missions – principally people and physical estate and buildings. The way that some businesses are responding to this challenge is by moving their cost base where possible from fixed to variable so that volume is not limited by infrastructure and, wherever possible, fixed costs are minimised.

The 'on demand' organisation focuses on core competencies and allows strategic partners to manage selected tasks. These partners should be able to provide this at high quality but lower transaction cost. They can do this because they are also offering the same services elsewhere – they are able to manage the peaks and troughs in demand that a single institution may not be able to absorb. Technology is the enabler that provides the necessary transparency and speed of delivery. In the above cases, the flexible demand might be met through delivering parts of the academic content or support electronically or from an alternate provider, or transferring some aspect of the course such as the mechanics of assessment.

One example of this is the high transaction operation for managing university admissions (via UCAS). This is an important activity with variable demand placed on it (currently increasing each year), and while universities could manage all the activity currently undertaken by UCAS themselves, from an operational perspective it is more efficient to outsource that aspect of the operation through a subscription service. The launch of new systems that link UCAS with universities in real-time and with digital transfer of all applicant information provides an example of on-demand activity in action. The paradox is that while the transactions that flow between universities and UCAS occur in real-time, the internal processes that take place within the university (because they are manual and rely on human intervention) can be time consuming and slow. So although the UCAS system is an effective way of outsourcing and dealing with multiple outcomes, volume change or the alteration of service needs, there is still a lack of integration across the application process as a whole. Within the context of FE, one college (see Box 9.2) improved information flows within the organisation by mass-scanning application forms, increasing its revenues from improved enrolment numbers, and improved the student experience by reducing waiting times for enrolment from two and a half hours to 14 minutes.

Universities and colleges are increasingly exploring how to extract additional value from what they already do at a more strategic level. So, as well as outsourcing, we can explore how to develop the services we are good at. There are examples of educational organisations extending teaching, learning and research services; providing accreditation services to other institutions; buying, selling and sharing educational content; exploiting intellectual property rights; offering academic administrative and other services and facilities beyond the organisation; and providing educational brokering services. One of the key new business models developing from the Web is the way it enables disparate, globally fragmented people and data to come together, brokered through specialist companies. Imperial College London, for example, found it had the critical mass and expertise to enable research knowledge transfer with major companies. It has now built on the experience developed so as to offer a service to smaller

Box 9.2 Project: student enrolment system

South Cheshire College wanted to streamline its student enrolment procedure. By adding an enrolment system to the existing MLE it also hoped to maintain its position as one of the country's leading colleges at inspection.

Process transformation and project implementation
There were three phases to the student enrolment implementation. The first phase was to put in place a system that enabled handwritten enrolment forms to be digitally processed by the College ICT system without any re-keying operations. The partners selected for this project included Campus IT in Dublin (MIS partner), RM (network management), and Canon who resourced high speed scanners at discounted prices.

The system scans students' handwritten forms into the College's electronic document management system for verification by staff. Single keystroke verification moves the information to the College's Student Record System which provides a 'fully collected student record'. There are no short entries. The whole process takes around 40 seconds.

Phase two was an online enrolment and payment system allowing students to select any course (that does not require an interview) from a home computer. The student completes a virtual form and makes payment via a secure and seamless link to Barclays Bank. The verification process takes seconds and, if successful, the enrolment confirmed.

The third phase, Web services interoperability, began with Campus IT and the College drawing up process maps which clearly showed if any divisions in labour existed. This phase resulted in the automatic creation of a student network account for the course and sets up a profile in the student record system. It gives the student access to the VLE, provides college and chat room email facilities, access to printers as well as peripheral benefits such as an online shop loyalty scheme.

Benefits
- When the system was first trialled the College increased its revenue by £30K over the six week Christmas period as students enrolled for part time courses. In 2005 this rose to £100K over the same period.
- Student enrolment reduced from queue based 2.5 hour manual process to average 14 minute process providing a massive saving in time and effort for students and staff.
- Students can begin course work immediately at point of enrolment.
- The system architecture is designed around the core MIS system. This enables partners to work on peripheral objects such as shop loyalty accounts without involving the College.
- Successfully added enrolment to its MLE to maintain position of country's leading college and succeeded with 13 Grade 1s at the most recent Grades inspection.

institutions who may lack that 'clout', providing them with valuable contact networks and support in matching with appropriate collaborators.

Here, we want to suggest that we can learn from the best e-business practices: first, by thinking through the whole range of possibilities across academic and administrative services both within and between post-compulsory educational institutions and second, by understanding the implications for customer focus, organisational integration and common standards. This also involves asking if buying-in or outsourcing e-learning materials or other services really does enable financial savings, enhances quality or adds value to a university 'brand'.

The how

Let us now consider how we get 'from here to there'. For a fully integrated e-business approach, the management team must determine the organisational structure best suited to the risk, capabilities, complexity, urgency and cost impact of each opportunity identified. There are at least four structures that might be considered, which enable such transformational developments to be effectively taken forward within large, complex organisations.

1 Embedded

Strategy and implementation are here orchestrated via a specialist cross-organisational innovations unit of some kind. An example of the embedded structure is provided by IBM, who set up a discrete internal Internet division in 1995. The head of this new division was tasked with ensuring every IBM product incorporated the new Web technologies. The division was focused on developing the 'white spaces' – empty spots where the company needed to develop new products with those products eventually embedded within existing divisions of the company. In the educational context, this could be a new internal administrative activity, which might be set up initially to develop online administrative transactions to develop solutions to student registration, course module changes, module registration or student loan activity, before moving to other areas highlighted by the initial analysis of business opportunities.

2 Separate structure

An example of a separate structure is provided by the retail financial sector, which set up new business units to exploit online banking (e.g. First Direct for HSBC and Egg for Prudential). These businesses were set up in a completely separate area from the traditional business with their own profit and loss statements. Without the hindrance of existing organisational or technology structures, such new 'organisations' are able to begin with a new framework, potentially exploit a lower cost base and to have the greater agility to move flexibly. In the educational context, this could be the creation of a new structure to deliver a brand new programme or course, or to exploit a new international market. Rather than developing a new physical campus to support the operation, it would be developed with a view to virtual rather than physical delivery of the service, perhaps exploiting portal technology for personalised and customised delivery of learning, research and administrative activity. Some US universities have deliberately used this route to set up online learning operations, without the complications of obtaining 'buy-in' from their existing academic and administrative staff (see Chapter 5).

3 Spin-out structure

In a combination of the previous two approaches, an innovative project is taken to a certain level within an organisation and then – if it proves itself – is expanded into a separate entity. An example is provided by Microsoft, which launched its online travel services product initially set up as a separate operating unit within Microsoft. In 1999, Microsoft spun off Expedia, raising $84 million in capital, with Microsoft retaining a controlling share of the stock. This enabled Expedia to then adopt an aggressive acquisition strategy purchasing both Travelscape.com and VacationSpot.com in 2000. In the educational context there are many examples of research activities that culminate in successful independent businesses, and it is possible to consider examples of a range of e-learning or other educational activities that might be developed and then exploited in this way. WebCT, for example, was originally developed as its own VLE by the University of British Columbia in Canada and then spun off into a successful, global business, which recently merged with Blackboard. Portal technologies provide another example, such as the successful portal development based at Case Western Reserve, which has been spun out as Campus EAI. This has been developed using a consortium open source approach to portal development with a not-for-profit operating model supported by a major technology partner (Oracle). It now has partners in the USA, UK and Australia, who collaborate on areas of common interest, avoiding the need for local development teams, and sharing the investment in new facilities.

4 Joint venture/collaboration

Finally, universities and colleges can work together as partners in project or process development. ChemConnect provides an example of this approach adopted by nearly all of the 25 largest chemical producers. This Internet chemical exchange was created to provide an open neutral marketplace for manufacturers, buyers and intermediaries to conduct online transactions for chemicals. This solution reduces product, transaction and distribution costs and with over 10,000 members now turns over in excess of $8 bn. The collaborative approach is well understood by educational institutions – one e-business example is London Universities Purchasing Consortium (already mentioned in Chapter 8), which models good practice in using a collaborative approach between different universities to achieve savings with online suppliers, for instance, for the supply of energy and laboratory materials to the universities.

Conclusion

E-business in education is still in its early stages, but models now exist for successful redesign and implementation of core processes; and out-tasking or sharing of secondary activities. A relatively small number of organisations have reached an advanced stage and there are a range of e-business projects and initiatives within the sector, some of which have been outlined throughout this book. There is much to be learnt from the lessons of the best e-business practices, but the potential gains for post-compulsory education will only be realised after considerable planning and management effort.

This leads to two final points. First, educational institutions, in moving forward from evolutionary stages to transformational stages (whether within individual projects, across a whole process, for all aspects of the organisation or across both inside and 'outside' collaborators), have to decide how to define the 'there' they want to get to. This is both in relation to market-oriented objectives and to public service intentions. Following (and adapting) Osterwalder and Pigneur (2002: 2), universities and colleges can examine:

1   The **products and services** they offer, providing an experience good of substantial value to the customer, for which they are willing to 'subscribe' and, if appropriate, other transactional products for which customers are willing to pay.
2   The structure and quality of **information and knowledge transfer processes** that underpin the services provided so as to ensure that appropriate content is accessible, customised and secure for all its different users.
3   The **infrastructure and the network of partners** that is necessary in order to create value, to maintain good customer and stakeholder relationships.
4   The **relationship capital** created and maintained with the customer and other stakeholders, in order to satisfy them, to support user loyalty and engagement and to generate sustainable revenues.
5   And last, but not least, the **financial aspects**, which are transversal and can be found throughout the three former components, such as cost and revenue structures.

Second, although it is the new Web-enabled technologies of ease and speed of data transfer that have enabled e-businesses such as Cisco and IBM to develop new approaches as to how they run themselves and to offer innovative business models to potential customers, these technologies are merely enablers not determinants of how universities and colleges can or should be operating. As Judy Evans, Senior Assistant Registrar (Management Information) University of Brighton, has noted, there are many concerns within the HE and FE sector that:

> software houses frequently develop solutions that customers have to force their operations into ... [this] is not the most appropriate way to develop an e-solution to business requirements. There has to be a greater degree of partnership in such developments, whilst recognising that many HEIs have to buy solutions 'off the shelf' as they cannot afford the enormous investment of 'bespoke' solutions'.[5]

Throughout this book, the focus has always been against simplistic technological 'solutions' and in favour of understanding and supporting specific educational and organisational processes. In this context, the kind of e-business approaches outlined here have hopefully opened up some additional avenues for consideration by senior managers and others in universities and colleges, who are looking for ideas to develop existing processes and systems towards more transformational uses of ICT.

As was said in the Preface, this book has not been about trying to suggest that the UK HE and FE sector should operate more like a commercial business. It *is* saying that universities and colleges can respond constructively to the intense commercial and other pressures they are now facing by exploiting the opportunities (and recognising the threats) offered by new technologies – in particular Web-enabled information transfer and communication. A critical understanding of e-business approaches is important to help meet the future challenges of post-compulsory education provision. In this way, hopefully, the sector can make innovative and effective changes, which meet student needs and reinvigorate itself in the process.

Notes

Special thanks to Nigel Herriott, Education and Research Client Executive IBM, for his help in the writing of this chapter.

1   See University of Warwick www.estrategy.warwick.ac.uk and www.warwick.ac.uk/pc, also University of Strathclyde www.strath.ac.uk/projects/sli/index.html.
2   See Buena Vista University eBVYou Program www.bvu.edu/~ebvyou.
3   See Case Western Reserve University Portal Development www.campuseai.org.
4   See University of North Carolina www.unc.edu/cci/index.html, www.ucisa.ac.uk/activities/awards/2001/travelburs/warwickreport.doc. And University of North Carolina at Chapel Hill http://its.unc.edu/.
5   J. Evans to Jos Boys, personal email comment, 13 September 2005.

Bibliography

Booz-Allen Hamilton Inc. (2006) 'Click-starting your organisation: how traditional companies are mobilizing for e-business'. Online. Available at www.boozallen.de/content/downloads/viewpoints/5K_ClickSta.pdf (accessed February 2006).

Osterwalder, A. and Pigneur, Y. (2002) 'An e-business model ontology for modeling e-business', 15th Bled Electronic Commerce Conference – e-Reality: Constructing the e-Economy (Bled, Slovenia), 17–19 June.

Palmisano, S. (2003) (IBM Chief Executive) keynote address to IBM Leadership Forum, November.

Index

added value 38, 40, 116–34, 119; of
tuition 123
administration 30–1, 57–8, 123, 140
admissions 27, 147, 148
applications 52
audits 116
augmented reality 133
Australian examples 58, 73, 97, 101,
123–4, 128, 130
authentication 16, 96

blended learning 9, 10, 20, 38, 55,
69, 73, 75, 78, 132
brand identity 52, 70, 71, 73, 84,
94, 123, 149

change: agents 141; levels of
technological 19–21; management
processes 103–5; in post-
compulsory education 88
changing: context 11–12;
environments 42–4, 88;
organisational relationships 44–5
Chinese examples 68–9, 73, 77–8, 84
collaboration 146; and mass-
customisation 25; and multi-media
learning 80–1; resistance to 96;
with external partners 40
common standards *see*
standardisation
competition 59, 73, 84, 137; in the
US 70–1; versus collaboration 3
competitive advantage 6, 94, 125
consortia 68–70, 78–9, 130, 151
consumption of educational services
51
content management systems 94
context aware computing 133

continuous professional development
3, 29, 70, 81, 129
corporate universities 12, 18
cost–benefit analysis 111–14;
problems with 111
cost of ICT 91–7, 105; evaluating
110–13
cost savings 35
customer: centredness 2, 35; focus 4,
38–42, 64, 76, 98–9, 125, 149;
interactive relationship 2; or
member 6, 125; perspective 40;
relationship management (CRM)
58, 64, 92, 120, 123–7; retention
10; service 14; student as 6

data: access to 6, 131; management
processes 2; real-time 58
Dearing Report 89–91
demand *see* supply and demand
Department for Education and Skills
e-strategy 75
distance learning 9, 54–6, 61, 69,
70–1, 79, 83, 99, 124, 132

e-business: definition 4, 21;
differences from mainstream
business 16–19; learning from 1–2,
33–48; models 60–3; shape of
34–8; strategy 141
e-commerce 17, 21, 56
e-learning 8–9, 11, 94, 95; in China
77–8; strategies 56, 107; take-up
95–6; trends 9; and success in the
US 74; and the University of
California 11
e-mail *see* email
e-procurement 40, 128, 139